A Woman Trapped in a Woman's Body
(Tales from a Life of Cringe)

A Woman Trapped in a Woman's Body

(Tales from a Life of Cringe)

Lauren Weedman

SASQUATCH BOOKS
SEATTLE

The chapters "Diary of a Journal Reader," "I'm Hugging You with My Voice,"
and "A Fatty-Gay Christmas" were first published, in slightly different form,
in Swivel magazine.

Publisher's note: Thanks go to Brangien Davis, who provided invaluable
editorial guidance as the manuscript was written, revised, and polished.

Printed in the United States of America
Published by Sasquatch Books
Distributed by PGW/Perseus
15 14 13 12 11 10 09 08 07   9 8 7 6 5 4 3 2 1

Cover photograph: David Belisle, in homage to Cindy Sherman, *Untitled Film
Still #7* (1978)
Cover design: Joan Zukor
Interior design and composition: Joan Zukor

Library of Congress Cataloging-in-Publication Data
Weedman, Lauren.
A woman trapped in a woman's body : tales from a life of cringe / Lauren
Weedman.
      p. cm.
      ISBN-13: 978-1-57061-501-6
      ISBN-10: 1-57061-501-2
   1. Autobiographical fiction, American. I. Title.

PS3623.E42W66 2007
813'.6--dc22
                                        2007020905

Sasquatch Books
119 South Main Street, Suite 400
Seattle, WA 98104
(206) 467-4300
www.sasquatchbooks.com
custserv@sasquatchbooks.com

To Sharon and Sid Weedman,

Happy fiftieth wedding anniversary—
please don't actually read this book

and

Jeff

CONTENTS

INTRODUCTION

The stories in this book are all half lies and exaggerations, yet completely true.

All names have been changed with the exception of a few that I forgot but am not worried about because none of them are the litigious sort.

UNDERMEDICATED:
A LOVE STORY

And here's your desk!"

Stephanie, the twenty-something office manager at *The Daily Show*, is gesturing toward the desk in the corner—a desk that is clearly someone else's. There is a sweater slung over the back of the chair with long dark hairs stuck to the collar. There are pictures of dark-haired people in front of Cape Cod–style houses. And there are stacks of scripts that say "Attn: Dark-haired Girl."

"But this is somebody's else's desk, right?" I ask.

"Well, technically, it kind of is. But she may not be coming back. But she may be."

"How about if I just sit next to the desk—I'll just use it if I need a hard surface."

Stephanie considers this for a moment and then makes an executive decision.

"No! I want you to go ahead and sit here. All the way. Go ahead, scoot your chair all the way in. But if you do see a woman who looks like—" she picks up a photo of dark-haired people hugging golden retrievers and points to the woman on the end, the only one without a golden retriever to hug—"this, then maybe just go ahead and get up and go sit over there." She gestures toward a stained and abandoned office chair in the corner of the room, facing the wall.

It's a slightly less glamorous beginning than I had imagined, but that doesn't matter because getting the job on *The Daily Show* is the most incredible thing that has ever happened to me. I will never know another unhappy day. Even bad days will be kind of good because I'll have health insurance. Like the Queen.

Finally, after all the years of striving, I can relax. No more living like a girl baby born to a Chinese family, having to prove that I am worth something. ("Please don't drown me in the river. I may not be strong and I may not be smart, but hand me that noodle and I'll make a joke with it. Please, let me live! Let me live!")

I am going to be allowed to live.

And not only that, my worth will be well established. Gone are the days of my telling every gross personal detail about herpes scares and porn-addicted boyfriends peeing in plants. I can now just sit quietly. Like the pretty girls do. (And the depressed girls.) Everything is going to change.

Stephanie whips around to continue her welcoming.

"Okay? So, first day! Exciting! Are you excited?"

"Yeah. I am," I say, making my way toward my corner. "So is this how you find out you're fired here? You just come in to work and someone else is at your desk? I think I'm just going to stand the whole time I'm working here."

Stephanie suddenly looks sad.

"I'm sorry I'm not laughing—it just takes *a lot* to make me laugh. It has to be like, hilarious, to make me laugh. I'm sure you're really funny, but I'd just be careful with the 'trying to be funny' thing. Everyone has a really low tolerance for that around here. So, anyway, welcome!"

With that Stephanie leaves the room. I wish I had not said that thing about being fired. Am I trying to "cut through the bullshit" on day one? Next I'll be asking why no black people work here.

One thing's for certain: I don't want to sit at that desk. Except to find clues as to why this *desaparecido* girl may or may not be coming back. I need to know what not to do. First, don't have dark hair, I got that. There must be other clues—evidence of certain herbs or supplements she had been taking, or journal entries that start with, "Said no to anal—Jon mad again."

Getting your dream job and then being let go. What a nightmare. And apparently when you're let go here it's just sort of "implied." ("Hmmm, that's weird. No paycheck for you again.")

Well, she's OUT and I am IN! So let's get back to the party that started three days ago, when I found out I got the job. You know what would be nice right about now? Another piece of celebration coffee cake, then maybe a gift basket.

I stare at the phone, imagining the congratulatory calls that are sure to come from the prominent figures from my past . . .

"Lauren! It's Mrs. Hart, and all the members of your third-grade class. We just called to say (here we go, everybody!), 1-2-3, CONGRATULATIONS!"

And then there will be the calls from my current life as well . . .

"Lauren, it's your father. Congratulations, good for you! Listen, you forgot to return the video you rented when you were here visiting. So you owe us twelve dollars for late fees. And your Uncle Noble died."

Back in reality, the phone rings—it's my manager.

"Hey, ya big fat famous noodle—how is the first day? We have to go celebrate tonight with cosmos and sushi."

I love my manager's wild streak but offer a gentle suggestion: "If you want we can wait to celebrate when you're not eight months pregnant."

"Oh please!" she says. "I'm a European mom. I'm sitting in the sauna stoned out of my mind, getting ready to shoot a porno! Ha ha ha!!! So how is it? Tell me, tell me, *tell me!*"

Someone knocks on the door.

"Oh fuck, someone's at the door," I say, looking for something to duck underneath.

"It's probably Jon Stewart. Get it! Get it!" my manager shouts.

I hang up and start self-fluffing. Come on, Lauren, get hard . . . get hard.

It's Stephanie. The bottom part of her face (from her adorable nose on down) is smiling and happy—full of hope. But the top half, particularly the "windows into her soul," didn't get the memo and is exuding "something has gone horribly wrong."

"Hey, they're gonna use you on the show tonight!" she says with the happy section of her head.

Then the phone rings.

"NO!" Stephanie yells at the phone. And for a moment her face comes together, then snaps right back. "Sorry—exciting first day, huh? Yeah, um, you can go ahead and get that."

It must be my manager calling back—probably hoping Jon is in the room and that maybe I'll put him on and when they hit it off she can have a quick fling before her baby is born.

Personally, I would never ask for a fling. "Soulmate" is more my secret hope. After watching tape after tape of *The Daily Show* to prepare me for the job (I'd never seen the show before I was hired, cable being as mystical and magical as health insurance), I had to agree with all the men, women, and stalkers. Jon is a charming, humble, political genius of a man.

Trying to be ironic and witty, I pick up the phone with a mock reporter voice:

"This is Lauren Weedman, new correspondent on *The Daily Show*. Can I help you?"

Long pause. Long, long pause.

"Oh . . . hi. I was just calling to get my messages. Who is this?"

It's 4 p.m.—rehearsal time—and I can't find the studio.

This morning Stephanie had told me something something something, turn right, then left. But every right turn runs me into a bagel buffet or cold cereal kitchenette and every left turn takes me into someone's secret mini Butterfingers stash or a bowl of brownies. The building is like a giant feedbag.

I'm really lost. It's 4:05. Shit. I'm going to have to go back up to my office and start again.

Why don't I just ask someone where it is? Why am I suddenly shy? I see a guy coming out of the writers' room by himself—he seems safe.

"Hello," I call out.

"You can just say 'Hi.' You don't have to be ironic about it," he says and walks away.

I finally find the studio on my own.

Even though I'm late, I take a brief moment to savor this momentous occasion. I am about to walk into *The Daily Show* studio for the first time. Pausing to reflect, I grab a mini Snickers from the bowl in the hallway and cram it into my mouth.

This is my first time meeting Jon—dear god, I hope I don't fuck this up.

When, at age nineteen, I first met my birth mother, my adoptive mother sent her a letter to help prepare her for me:

> *Dear Diane,*
> *Thank you for our beautiful daughter! She has given us literally hours of entertainment. But Lauren can also be quite a handful. She tends to live only for today with never a thought for tomorrow! This has made her life—and ours!—very difficult at times. She is also very bad with money. If left unmonitored she will nickel and dime herself to death!*

My spending habits are not what Jon should be warned about—somebody should probably warn him that sometimes I'm not funny, and now I'm being paid to be funny. Which suddenly seems like an intense amount of pressure. I'm going to end up like John Belushi or Chris Farley by the end of the week. Minus the legend part. Just bloated with drugs and alcohol and mini Snickers. But I'm not always funny. Sometimes I'm tired.

That's kind of funny, I think. I'm gonna say that when I walk in the studio.

Upon opening the studio door I find a circle of men throwing around a Nerf football, one of whom is Jon Stewart. Nobody even turns his head when I walk in. Maybe I should start crying. No, I'll save that for my second season. As soon as I see Jon I want to tell him my story about my boyfriend peeing in the houseplant, show him the tuft of hair by my ankle that I always miss when I'm shaving, and then, oh my god, I want to nickel and dime myself to death.

I remind myself: You're an oak tree—your roots run deep and your skin is barky—just be rooted and present. Remember, like grizzly bears, these guys are more scared of you than you are of them. It's a comedy show—have fun! Yukka, yukka, banana peel, whoa! Come on! We're all just folks—folks are folks—we live, we die, we rot. Jon Stewart is just a man—he's just a man—and you've had so many men before, in so many ways—he's just one more. Oh my god, it's a song lyric from *Jesus Christ Superstar*—I've turned Jon Stewart into Jesus.

Right as I'm about to belt out the alto line, "What's the buzz, tell me what's a-happening!" the men spot me and stop throwing the ball.

I run in (holding my breasts since I'm not wearing a jog bra) as if I were late for the game. I squeeze myself into the circle, throw my hands above my head, and scream, "I'm open! I'm open!"

And I mean it. Open to new friends, new experiences, new anything.

But the game comes to a complete stop.

That's when I notice that Jon has the ball. (It's not until later that I realize he always has the ball.)

He greets me with a worried "Hi, Lauren. How're ya doing?"

"I'm just . . . dealing with all the . . . sexual . . . tension." (Pause.) "You know . . . Fine. I'm fine."

"Good. It's good to see you. We'll be starting rehearsal in about twenty minutes," he says with a look on his face that is not amused surprised, as I'd initially interpreted, but fear.

The first time I'm on the show, I'm assigned a bit where I'm an entertainment expert talking about which of the Backstreet Boys is the gay one, which is the really gay one, and which is the really, *really* gay one.

In the studio you do one rough run-through, where you're bad and you flub your words and then squeegee the sweat off your eyebrows and do it again. The first one is a stumble-through, and it is petrifying. Since I had originally auditioned for the executive producer, rather than for Jon, it is also the first time that the star of the show is seeing me "act like a reporter."

I complete the first run-through and immediately begin an inner mantra like a screaming army sergeant: "YOU'RE OKAY! YOU'RE OKAY! THAT WAS THE FIRST TIME—GIVE YOURSELF A BREAK!"

Then I feel the ground rumbling. A herd of comedy writers is making its way toward me and soon I'm surrounded by urgent suggestions. One writer steps out in front of the mob only to be shoved out of the way by someone even more desperate to save his joke from the new girl.

"Lauren! Okay . . . how can I explain this—"

"Just tell her what you want."

"Okay, you're an expert. Meaning you know what you're talking about. Have you ever seen Stone Phillips?"

"Don't confuse her. Maybe she doesn't understand exactly what the joke is. Underline it in the script!"

"She doesn't understand. Let me try. Hey, Lauren! Whassup! You look great! Pretty hair!"

"We don't have this kind of time. We need to give it to a Steve!"

At which point the entire studio erupts in a chant: "Steve! Steve! Steve!"

I join in. "STEVE! STEVE! STEVE!"

After learning that both Steves are on vacation we do one more run-through before the actual taping. It is even worse than the first one because suddenly I can't remember how to keep my eyeballs from shaking. I decide the best thing to do is to suck my cheeks in, nod a lot, and look angry yet insecure. The "just be yourself" technique. This seems to give the writing staff the comfort of knowing "that's as good as she's going to get," and they leave me alone during the actual taping.

The next morning the executive producer asks me, "Where'd you go after the show? Jon wanted to congratulate you but you just disappeared. I think he was worried you were upset."

Normally I wait to make sure everyone is looking at me before I storm out of a building in tears, but this time I'd forgotten to check over my shoulder. And Jon had noticed. Oh my god. I love him.

"You are my new boyfriend," I say, sticking my head into Jon's office. He looks surprised to see me. He's on the phone with Wolf Blitzer. At least, I assume it's Wolf Blitzer because he says, "I'll talk to you later, Wolf," and hangs up. It could have been Wolfman Jack. He's dead, but Jon can get anyone on the phone.

I notice Jon's Emmy is on a shelf, still wrapped in plastic.

"Look how modest you are, Jon," I say. "You haven't even unwrapped your Emmy."

Jon brings the conversation back under his control.

"Hey, great job on the show last night," he says. "Welcome. I didn't see you after the show, so I wanted to make sure you were feeling okay."

"Thank you. I appreciate that," I reply. And that should be the moment I leave, but I don't.

"I just love that you don't have a special cabinet built for your awards. Everyone I know with a bowling trophy has special spotlights installed—giant arrows on the wall pointing to it. Naked women dancing around it. That's what you should get."

Jon looks confused, but he continues to keep his concern focused.

"Well, Lauren. We're glad to have you here. I just wanted to tell you that after the taping."

"You know what happened after the show?"

Jon glances at the clock on the wall and takes a breath. But I am oblivious to his "I don't have time; I've reached out to you, now please let me get some work done" signals.

"I walked out of the studio and immediately started sobbing."

He makes sad eyes that say, "Oh no!" and then looks at his phone. Probably praying for Kofi Annan or Carrot Top to call him. But until they do, I continue.

"It's just intense. I've never been on national television before, and the stakes were so high. I had to get out of the building and let all the stress out. I went in the alley to have a private breakdown but ended up sobbing in front of the doors where the audience exits. So suddenly the doors fly open: 'Hey, there's the new girl! Great job!' and I'm trying to stop crying—"

I finally stop myself because I realize Jon has a "that's a sad story" look frozen on his face, but his eyes are darting from the phone to the clock to the door. The phone, the clock, the door. The phone, the clock, the door.

I start to laugh and hope he'll join me. But somehow he doesn't see the humor in a new hire telling him that she may or may not be stable.

We very formally end our conversation with some "welcome agains" and "I'm exciteds" and "thank yous."

The journey to my office is always exhausting. Every time I pass an open office door I stick my head in and try to say something funny. I try to convince myself that I'm just saying hi. Getting to know the people of *The Daily Show*. By the end of the first week, it's turned into a bizarre dance routine.

Step, step, look right, "OK, guys—hands outta your pants!"

Step, step, look left, "Man, crack cocaine makes you sweat a lot, look at you!"

Step, step, look right, "For a fat person you're looking very thin today."

Ball change and repeat.

If the person responds or laughs I take that as an invitation to come on in and ask them for advice. I want to know what the women before me have done. And why everyone keeps saying, "It's sooo hard to keep women here." But people just nod and smile at me and reveal nothing. Which may have to do with the fact that they're "working."

One month later, I'm back in the executive producer's office.

"Okay, I don't want to freak you out," she is saying. "I want to help you. Here's the deal. You need to get Jon to like you."

"I wasn't aware that he didn't," I respond, in an unemotional, I-could-care-less-about-this-job, it's-a-walk-in-the-park tone.

She continues: "Somehow he's getting the impression that you could care less about the job. He feels like you're treating this whole thing like it's a walk in the park. Like you could take it or leave it. And we all like you but we need him to like you too, so—"

Just then someone opens her office door. It's Jon, sticking his head in. I throw up a little bit in my mouth. Then swallow it. Then hope it won't affect my breath in case Jon wants to give me a hug.

The executive producer's voice goes up a few octaves. "Hey, Jon, come on in! I was just talking to Lauren about how excited we are to have her as a part of the show. Just telling her to try to relax and have fun."

Jon nods his head and very politely says, "Yeah. Good. Listen, can I talk to you when you're done with Lauren?"

I jump to my feet, put my hands on my hips, pinch my nipples, and say, "I just want to please you. Do I please you, Jon? Do I?"

Jon looks at the executive producer and seems like he's about to say something. Since he doesn't laugh I figure I'd better start dancing like Shirley MacLaine—as fast as I can.

"Jon! I think that my nervousness—trying to act like this isn't the biggest thing that's ever happened to me—is backfiring. It's like when I first started dating my husband, I tried to act like I was used to sexy, gorgeous men. Which in my mind meant acting very cool and underwhelmed. I'm so worried about you licking me—what is wrong with me?—I mean *liking* me—"

"Is she serious?" Jon asks the executive producer.

She tells him that I'm kidding. She speaks for me a few more times before I say, doing my best deaf person imitation and using sign language, "Tell Jon I like his shirt."

The executive producer bursts out laughing. "Oh my god!" she exclaims. "Girlfriend, you've got to get us all what you're on! Oh my god! Okay, Jon, I'll be in your office in a minute."

She continues to laugh until Jon closes the door behind him. The instant it clicks shut, she leaps toward me, grabs my arm, and starts shaking me.

"You have got to calm down!" she says. "Stop auditioning for the job! Relax!"

Am I acting so differently from the way I normally do? This is just me, right?

When I was six years old, my mom set me up to play with a foster kid named Fritz from down the street. At that age, the difference between "adopted" and "fostered" wasn't clear to me—they were both said with a sad whisper. So the day I found out that Fritz had been considered "a handful" and that his foster parents had *sent him back* was more than mildly traumatizing. Poor Fritz had clearly not provided his new family with hours of entertainment. From the day of his deportation on I started performing at least ten minutes of stand-up comedy a day at the dinner table.

Now, standing in front of the bulletin board in the hallway, I scan all the sign-up sheets for softball games and trips to Vegas and free tickets to stand-up shows to see if Jon's name is anywhere. One of the other on-air correspondents walks by and I ask him if Jon ever plays softball and he laughs in my face. He recovers and decides to share the secret to his success on the show.

"You need to stop treating Jon like a peer," he says. "He's not your peer. Just lay low until they want to use you on the show. Don't ask for too much feedback. You're just calling attention to yourself. And don't sign up for anything on this board. On-camera people don't do that."

A producer on his way to pick up his antidepressants stops and joins in. "And don't laugh so much. I didn't laugh at anything for the first year I worked here. So when I finally did, it really meant something."

I'm in the studio for rehearsal. I should be practicing my lines but instead I'm practicing not laughing. Starting with not laughing at my own jokes (which, for me, embarrassingly, is incredibly difficult).

As soon as Jon walks in, everyone quiets down and gets focused.

"Don't spin around in the chair," the stage manager whispers to me, trying to help. "Just sit still."

Jon has brought his new puppy, who's jumping all over the crew.

"Sorry about my puppy, you guys, he's going through a licking stage," he says.

"I wish my husband had one of those!" I exclaim, careful not to burst out laughing. The studio falls silent and then, in the Jewish tradition of ripping one's clothing to signify "you are dead to me," the studio is full of the sound of collars being torn.

I've only been on the show for six months and I've been banished from sitting next to Jon in the studio. "You're too jumpy, you make him nervous," I'm told.

They have me work almost exclusively in the field, finding mildly retarded people who don't have cable so they'll never know how much the show makes fun of them.

Sometimes I enjoy myself. Dripping wax on my breasts at an Amish candle-making studio for a "Wild on Amish Country" piece is memorable. Not for my parents, but I enjoy it.

Interviewing a tobacco lobbyist whose wife and child had just left him and moved out the day before is less fun. Mocking is one of my favorite pastimes, but this is rough. He makes the entire crew lunch and plays with his dog on camera, which we ask him to do because he looks so ridiculous doing it. He rolls around on the ground with snorty abandon.

In the van, driving away, I feel like a bully. The guy is a tobacco lobbyist, for god's sake—he deserves to have his eyeballs colored in red and horns drawn on his head. So why do I feel like I've just gone up to the fattest girl in high school (which could have been me, though technically I was the twelfth fattest, but was heavily girdled) and told her that the cool kids wanted her to come to a movie with us? And did it in such a way that she took a chance and joined us at the movie. But of course we'd only asked her so we could mock the shit out of her. And it wouldn't be until the next day at school (or the "air date"), when we'd be reporting how she ate nachos with her chubby fingers, that she'd realize she'd been set up.

You'd think after so many years of having my metaphorical lunch money stolen, I'd be pleased to finally get cast in the role of bully with health insurance. But I wasn't. I missed jumping up and down in my chair next to Jon.

Like most workplace dramas, my situation came to a head, as it were, with the Giant Black Cock (GBC) incident.

There are no sexual harassment lawsuits in comedy. Maybe because there are so few women around to get offended. ("Did he mean *my* pubic hair? Hey!") And "just kidding" works in every situation.

So when the first thing that greets me on my computer screen one morning is a picture of a white blond chirpy (WBC) enjoying a GBC, I know exactly how this day is going to go.

My job is to march around the office trying to find out who did it and pretending I'm going to press charges. (Since there are no black people working on *The Daily Show* I don't have to worry about someone saying, "It's not mine.")

By the end of the day there is only one person whom I have not yet asked about the GBC. And I find that person conveniently trapped in his makeup chair, right before the show.

"Jon, was it you who downloaded the giant black cock onto my computer?" I ask.

Jon looks truly shocked. This is the same guy who sat around making jokes with the writers about grandmas falling on young men's dicks, and now he's looking at me like I've taken a shit in my hand and offered it to the Pope.

"What are you talking about, Lauren?"

The makeup lady looks like she is about to cry.

"I came in to work and there was a picture of this giant black cock on my computer, and normally it's my mom who sends me those pictures but—"

He stands up and thanks the makeup lady and walks out.

The makeup lady, who has been working with Jon since he was on MTV, says, "I think you need to go and have a heart-to-heart with him. He thinks you're making fun of him or something. He can't tell that you're kidding, I think. I've known him a long time and I just think he doesn't get your kidding. I would go right now and talk to him. Like how you talk to me. Like how you talk to everyone but him. Just as yourself."

I know she's right. This has gone on for too long. I knock on the door of the green room.

BAM BAM BAM. People respond to truth. I want to tell him my truth.

BAM BAM BAM. The Lord has sent me. Open up.

BAM BAM BAM. Listen. Fritz got sent back because of me! I set him up. He asked if he could have one of my dad's pennies from his penny jar, and I said, "Yes! Take it!" Then Fritz returned to his foster home and they checked his pockets and found the penny. When my mother asked me, "Did you tell Fritz he could have the penny?" I told her, "No! I didn't! He stole it! Something is wrong with that kid! He's bad, I tell ya, BAAAAD!"

When Jon finally says, "Come in," I walk into the room to find him surrounded by all his people. Every single one of the eight important people in the room looks at me as if I have a bomb strapped to my torso.

"Jon," I say, certain of my mission. "I want to talk to you for minute. Could you come out in the hallway, please?"

Jon doesn't smile or try to smile or act patient. He is done with that shit. He says, "What? Out there?" He actually starts to stand up, and then hangs in midair above his chair as he changes his mind. "No, I'm not going out there. What do you want?"

I dive in. "Jon, every time we have an interaction I hear the next day that I've upset you. And I don't know what it is. No matter what I do I just make it worse and worse. And I don't mean to. I honestly keep thinking that I'm being myself but somehow—"

Jon stops me. "Lauren, you strike me as a very obsessive person. You need to calm down. I don't know what you're talking about. I don't think about you or our interactions as much as you seem to."

And I shut up because I get it. My muscles unclench. My heart rate slows and I get it.

It's like I've been running after Jon for a year, asking, "Does this shirt smell? Does it? Tell me, tell me!" And now he's told me, quite honestly. It's liberating. I feel free and ready to start doing some actual work.

Enjoying this new sense of relaxation and ease, looking forward to how well I'll finally sleep tonight, I calmly turn around and begin to close the door behind me. But before the door has completely shut I stick my head back in.

"You mean you don't think about me on the weekends?" I say. "I think about you . . . "

Three weeks later, I call in to retrieve my voicemail and a strange woman answers my phone.

"Oh . . . hi," I say, after a long pause. A long, long pause. "I was just calling to get my messages. Who is this?"

EMMYS

Seven months after 9/11, things in New York are still touch and go. There's a lingering feeling of unease in the air, and it seems like every time I look at the clock it says 9:11. I have my job on *The Daily Show* though, and neurosis and fear breed some amazing comedy (case in point—Buddy Hackett). But at this point in time (9/11 + 7) I am, along with the rest of the staff, just one loud door slam away from sobbing in a bathroom stall and eating my own hair. Which is not (yet) comedy we can market to our target audience of males ages eighteen through twenty-eight. They want the kind of comedy where a piece of poop comes to life and becomes an action hero. Nothing too reality-based right now. They are not alone. I, too, want out of this reality. Where are you, SuperPoo Man? Save me . . .

Walking into work I stop by my mailbox to see if my lesbian fan in Brooklyn has written me with updates about the website she's working on: ChicksWhoDigChicksWhoDig Weedie.com. But she hasn't. I wish my one fan wasn't so lazy. I've been waiting for the website to be up for months, acting like I couldn't be more annoyed by the whole thing while secretly feeling frustrated she isn't moving more quickly. Everyone else's fans drive them crazy, stalk them, etcetera. Mine has no follow-through. The only piece of mail in my box is a memo I received a few months back and left in my slot so it wouldn't look so completely empty. It's Comedy Central's "How to Deal with Post-Traumatic Stress Disorder" handout, which only reminds me of what I missed out on during the first weeks after 9/11—the weight loss and the "Why not? The world is ending!" promiscuous sex that everyone was having. Instead, I gained fifteen pounds and was begging my husband to "please, just blow on it, clear the cobwebs out, that's all—then you're done."

When I arrive at work, I find Mary, the production assistant, at her desk and in the middle of a visual gag—a scathing commentary on the officewide obsession with personal water bottles. She has taken one of the giant plastic jugs that usually supplies the water cooler and has written in large letters on the side, "MARY'S WATER BOTTLE." It's casually placed on her desk, taking up the entire surface, as she tries to get her work done around it. As I walk by she grabs it and hoists it up to her mouth using both arms. Two hours later, when we're both done laughing, she asks me if I've heard about the big announcement: We're going to the Emmys.

During the past seven months I've been careful not to feel anything from the nose up or the neck down. So upon hearing this news, all I'm able to squeeze out of my chin is a small, reserved, "That's exciting." I'm afraid to get excited about a fluffy, braggy, American thing because if I do the evildoers will get us. Then again, if I think that way, "They've won." And I'd rather win—for best comedy show.

Not that going to the Emmys was ever a childhood dream of mine. Winning an Oscar for playing Annie in the movie *Annie* had been my main concern. And "a trip to the Emmys" didn't make the cut this past New Year's Eve, when I did a ritual with a circle of sage-smoking women where we all had to write down our Dreams for the Coming Year. (They should have called it what it ended up being: Everyone But Lauren Write the Word "Peace" on a Slip of Paper. I would have added "peace" to my long list, too, but the paper was so small, and I just didn't have room in between "health insurance" and "the ability to love without slander.")

By the time I reach my office I've gone from "I don't really think about shallow things like award shows" to looking for babies to step on to get my name on the list of confirmed guests.

Between my normal work activities of wandering around searching for new snack options and finding new people to listen to me explain how hard it is to be married to a bartender, I notice that nobody is acting excited about going to the Emmys, but everyone is—without a doubt—going.

I remember how a few days after the eleventh there had been a staff meeting to talk about how much time it would take before we could be funny again. The state of shock in the room made it hard to get the discussion going, so in the meantime we were all instructed to try and find stories that involved soft and comforting things, like Amish people. And they had to be local Amish people, not Amish people that required an airplane trip to get to. Even the word "airplane" made our stomachs plop into our laps. Nobody wanted to take the subway—much less fly—ever again. We all decided that for the rest of our lives we would do like Loretta Lynn and the morbidly obese do: wrap a fried biscuit and a stick of butter in a plastic bag and take the bus. There were no circumstances that could ever justify taking what was now a nightmarish mode of transportation. Nobody was flying. Ever. Again.

Unless it was to the National Television Academy's 53rd Annual Primetime Emmy Awards.

The intercom system blasts an announcement through the building: "All staff needs to stop by Mary's desk to get your

Emmy tickets and limo assignments. And Lauren Weedman, please report to the executive producer's office right now."

As the gods of television broadcasting would have it, my contract is up for renewal the same day the limo assignments are being made for the Emmys.

When I walk in the executive producer's office, she has a look on her face that says, "Well, I tried . . . " She offers me a freelance contract and a hit of pot. I accept both and give her a big hug. Ask her how her son is doing. Where she got her shirt. How much weight has she lost. Did she end up getting that cabin? Can I get one more hug?

Next thing I know I'm outside her office door, thinking that was a good meeting. Now I'll have more time to do other projects, plus I'm still on the show. It's kind of perfect.

The first person I run into after the meeting is my good friend and field producer, Carrie, and her dog, Fred, both of whom had been evacuated to New Jersey on the eleventh. She's my "What do you want me to do—lie to you?" friend. She's let me know that one of the issues that got in the way of my success on the show was that, though talented, I just wasn't as cute as the other female reporters. Carrie clarified this by explaining, "I'm not saying that *I* don't think you're cute. I'm just talking about guys, the fans of the show, The American People and all the Comedy Central executives." She was painfully honest, and I have to admit, I trusted her. (Or I hated myself—tough call.)

"They offered me a freelance contract," I say and start to clap my hands to help get the applause going.

"That means you're fired," Carrie says, with not a hint of emotion in her voice. Unless exhaustion counts as an emotion.

"But why wouldn't they just tell me I'm fired?"

"They don't want to hurt your feelings. I'll go tell everyone we're going out to have a 'Lauren's been canned' drink after work. Come on, Fred."

It occurs to me that perhaps, as is often the case with Carrie, she's just doing what they'd taught her in preschool—to share whatever she had a lot of, whether it be Jolly Ranchers or bitterness. Maybe she doesn't really know whether I'm fired. She just wants to keep me down so she can look cheerful in comparison to someone who may have just been fired.

I reach down to pet Fred, trying to get a little comfort, but he yanks his head away.

"He only likes full-time employees," Carrie says.

"Me too," I whine.

"I'm kidding, geez. Sensitive. Are you going to be a mess at the 'Lauren's been canned' party? Because that's what everyone is gonna be scared of. So try not to be. We like a cheerful fired girl. Come on, Fred."

The next three random people I pass on the way back to my desk tell me the same thing. "That means you're fired. They just don't want to be mean."

The fourth person I pass is Mitch, a full-time comedy writer whose contract was also up for renewal. I know because he was called in to the office directly after me. He tells me they offered him a freelance contract too. And he's smiling. So you see, maybe it's not what Carrie says. And all those other people. Maybe it's exactly how it sounds.

"Yeah, freelance. So what do you think?" I ask him.

"No fucking way," Mitch says. "That's a joke. I just quit as soon as she offered it. I'm not stupid. I would never accept a deal like that."

After work, the few employees who aren't whooping it up at Mitch's "I told them to fuck themselves" party sit at a corner table for my "Sorry you got canned" party. Carrie tactfully asks the four other employees who've shown up if I'll be allowed to go the Emmys now that I'm not a full-time employee.

"They already invited me! They can't uninvite me!" I say.

"Yes they can!" the entire bar answers in unison.

The next morning I run up to Mary, who is wearing what she claims to be Snoop Dogg's underwear on her head, and ask her if I am still going to the Emmys. She rolls her eyes. Pats me on the head. Makes the sign for "she's gone cuckoo!" and says, "You nut! Of course you are! How could you not go—you're a part of the show! Why would you suddenly not be going?"

"Well, the freelance contract thing . . . "

"Freelance contract!" she says, pulling the underwear off her head. "You're on freelance contract? When did this happen? Um, I have to take Jon's puppy on a walk. We'll talk about this later."

She puts the underwear back on her head and walks straight into the executive producer's office. Which is not where Jon keeps his puppy.

Two days later I get a call from my manager, saying, "You're not going." Then I am going. Then I'm not going. Then I am. Then I'm tall. Then I'm short. Then I'm black. Then I'm white. Then I am going again. Then I'm not. Again. (As I told a co-worker, I'm just glad this isn't how the Make-A-Wish Foundation is run.) Finally my manager calls to tell me that the security guy's second cousin has backed out and I can have his ticket.

"Will your husband be joining you?" Mary asks, after I give her the news.

I wish Mathew could hear her say that. He and I have argued many times over the fact that whenever he meets anyone at my job they always give a little shocked jump, clasp their heart, and exclaim, "Husband? Lauren, you're married?" If he'd heard Mary's question he'd see that things were really changing in our marriage. Maybe he wouldn't even notice the way she put air quotes around the word "husband."

"Oh no, he's not going," I answer. And then I remember that you're supposed to *try* in a marriage. I correct myself:

"Oops, that sounded bad. What I meant to say is, does he get a free ticket?"

"We'd pay for his ticket to the ceremony but he'd have to pay for the rest."

"Then I don't think so. It's not really his thing."

That evening when I tell Mathew that I'm going to go to the Emmys and he isn't, he hangs his head and says, "Man, you are lucky. This may sound dumb, but it's like a childhood dream of mine."

Ow, my heart. Or maybe it's my irritable bowel syndrome. Whatever it is, it hurts.

Forever getting it wrong—that's how our marriage is starting to feel. I'm vaguely aware of how a loving person acts. I've seen it in the movies. I should insist that he go—remind him that money is never the issue and that it just won't be as much fun without him. But I want him to push more, to say, "I'm going, dammit," then punch me or something. Be forceful. Maybe not the punch (save that for our anniversary). We are constantly testing to see how much the other one really wants to be here. And every time the answer seems to be "not that much." Then again, how much more clear a message than "it's a childhood dream of mine" did I want?

I don't know what is wrong with us. I don't know why since 9/11, when everyone else has been growing closer to loved ones, Mathew and I have been freaking out in our own little individual cages. The only time we come together is when I stop by the bar where he works.

In the past the bar had been an environment that worked well for our relationship. Mathew stood safely behind the bar and I got drunk. Everybody wins! But recently things have become odd. As soon as I walk into the bar he makes these huge efforts to show me special attention. He'll introduce me to the other drunks in the bar as his beautiful wife ("Has everyone met my beautiful wife?"), which is a kind thing to say, I get that. And I don't immediately yell, "What the fuck is that about?" But somehow his voice sounds wrong. It sounds like it has been sounding more and more since we watched the buildings come down.

Right after we witnessed what felt to me like seeing the moon explode, he turned to me and said something like, "This day will go down in history," in a sort of FDR voice. He's used that old-fashioned radio announcer voice quite a bit since that day. "Somebody will pay a price for this . . . " "Four score and seven years ago . . . " He either talks to me in a rapid series of war cliches, or he talks about myriad topics that I judge as far too shallow considering the post-9/11 world we are now living in.

But just as I decide to make an effort and explain the details of what it would take for him to come with me to the Emmys, Mathew grabs his lighter and his cigarettes, chains his wallet to his belt, and whisks out of our tiny punishment of a New York apartment.

"I'll be back around 6:00 a.m.," he says, as he kisses the air just above my angry, abandoned, Emmys-bound face.

After weeks of shopping, I grow tired of store owners never believing that I'm going to the Emmys. Not one minor designer or random salesperson offers to donate a dress to the cause, despite my assurances that if we win—and we always do!—I'd be getting major camera time.

The dress I end up with is one that has been hanging in my closet for years and is appropriate for no occasion except something like the Emmys. I got it from Goodwill—but from their annual Glitter Sale, not the free bin. There wasn't any dried throw-up and wig hairs stuck to it (at least not before I got it). It was a lovely black Tinkerbell dress from the '50s that looked a bit like it had been hand-sewn for a high school play. (A private high school.)

I try the dress on for Mathew. Which I realize after the fact is a little cruel—sort of like the cameraman enjoying a sandwich as he photographs a child dying of starvation. Mathew likes the dress but asks me if it feels a little tight. I would answer but I can't get enough air into my squashed lungs to say "yes."

Undeterred, I figure what post-traumatic stress failed to do for me, Dr. Atkins will. This year, Atkins is the weight loss plan of choice for most city folk. There is this constant parade of people in a state of ketosis, running by with platters stacked with cheeses and ham and steak, and cubes of fat and gristle and oil muffins with hot oil filling. They breathe their blue-cheese breath on me as they gush, "God, and all this energy! I don't know what to do with it!" (Maybe have your tongue scraped?)

Before joining the ketosis brigade, my main concern about Atkins was digestive. "Will I poop?" I asked his constituents. ("Oh yes, this diet is perfect for that! I can't stop! Look at that—just talking about it, whoops, gotta go!")

I haven't pooped to my satisfaction in twenty years. Maybe thirty. Growing up, my mom made a chart next to the toilet where I was supposed to monitor my poops. Happy faces for good ones, sad faces for painful ones, faces with no features at all—just a round circle—for when I thought I had to go and nothing happened. Over the years people have tried to help me, giving me advice about getting it going. My friend Gay Jay once bought me a very expensive gift of colon cleansers that were supposed to unstick that bean burrito from 1974.

So I've been doing Atkins for three weeks now and I feel sick and shaky all the time. But all the women in Manhattan—who treat any waiter coming toward them with a bread basket like a date rapist: "NO! NO MEANS NO!"—tell me not to give up and to give it at least two months.

At the end of a very sad, weak workout at the gym I hop on the scale in the dressing room. You'd think after witnessing so much in the past year I would have gained some life perspective, but when I see what that fucking scale is telling me I scream and hit it with both of my hands, which causes my towel to fall off. Then I burst into tears and end my workout on the floor of the shower sobbing like Glenn Close in *The Big Chill*. The only difference is that she was crying because her friend had died and I am crying because I've gained two pounds. Besides that, the similarities are eerie.

It's day five of "no movement" when we're finally boarding our flight for the Emmys. But for once my bowels are not my major issue of the day. Flying has trumped pooping.

I've always been a giddy and petrified flyer. I prefer to sit by someone who is dressed like a pilot or flight attendant so I can keep my eye on them to make sure they don't suddenly make the sign of the cross.

Nuns, newborns, newlyweds clutching each other during takeoff, youth groups returning from or en route to building libraries in South America—anything reeking of "when bad things happen to good people" really frightens me.

Comedy Central people dominate our JetBlue flight from JFK to Long Beach. If we do go down, the entire staff—except Jon (hmmm)—will be wiped out.

The plane ride is much like the bus trip in the movie *One Flew Over the Cuckoo's Nest*. Everyone's medication is a little off today.

We're taxiing for takeoff and one of the writers has actually gotten out of his seat and is walking toward the front of the plane. I should have known he was a terrorist, he's always been so withdrawn and overly polite. The flight attendant yells at him over the intercom, "Sir! Sit down! You can't—"

He yells back, "You told me I could sit by my wife during takeoff! To wait until everyone was seated and then I could—"

She hangs up and comes storming toward him. "You can't stand up during taxi! Sit down!"

He doesn't seem to give a shit. He's just gotten married and is worried about his wife, who is nervous about takeoff. I've been married for three years and didn't even bring my husband with me . . . having decided that "it's my childhood dream" was a passive-aggressive statement.

I've ridden in a lot of planes but I've never seen someone get up during taxi and fight about it. And here I am, seeing it happen, and it's someone I know. The flight attendant gives him the "we're going to have to turn this plane around" spiel, but he keeps fighting.

"But you told me you'd come and get me after everyone was seated and I could—"

"I'm going to have to call the pilot and tell him—"

"But you said—"

I'm seated very close to all of this and it's freaking me out. The insanity does not die down once we reach our cruising altitude. We're a group of scared, alcoholic, post-9/11 New York comedy people, so as soon as turbulence starts the flight attendant bell is going off every three minutes.

Ding! "Is this normal? This amount of turbulence?"

"Oh yes. This is actually light chop. Pilots are trained to handle much heavier—"

Ding! "Is everything okay?"

"Yes, this is perfectly normal light chop."

Ding! "Does this mole look irregular to you?"

After a while everyone is making their way to the bathroom, weaving their way past me, clutching the seatbacks or the sweaty bald foreheads of their co-workers to make it to the lavatories.

It's a plane full of Woody Allens, without their foster wives to calm them down.

Maybe it's the LA heat, but that night in the hotel room, I try on my dress and it's still a little tight. In fact it's more than a little tight. There are areas of friction under my arms and slicing pain around my waist. Once the dress is fully zipped up, I'm running around the hotel room, screaming, "Get it off me! Get it off! I can't breathe! It's cutting me! It burns!"

Thanks to Dr. Atkins, my insides are packed full of salami and cheese. Very uncomfortable. In fact, upon landing in LA, I called Gay Jay (who lives in the area) and told him that I needed some sort of emergency evacuation.

He told me that I needed to talk to his yoga-Scientology friend, Saranella, who was really into this kind of thing. Jay reported that she recently did a coffee enema and has been glowing ever since.

Saranella is driving forty minutes to meet me in a Rite Aid parking lot to help me with my Emmys prep. It is instantly apparent that LA folks are much more on board with the Emmys thing than New Yorkers. They get it. It's nothing to be ashamed of here. It's like this city's prom. They don't roll their eyes or try to act unimpressed—they'll leave their children unattended in the bathtub if you call with an Emmys-related emergency. I imagined Saranella running out of her house, her husband holding a crying baby, saying, "Saranella, but it's our anniversary! The reservation is in thirty minutes!" And Saranella responding, "Can't talk. Gotta go! Emmys! Enema! Atkins! Filled with cheese—I'll explain later!"

Once we gather at Rite Aid, Saranella says, "So here's what you need, an enema bag, a hot water bottle with a rubber hose attached, and some good magazines." She's so excited for me. "You're gonna have the movement of your life!" she says. "I'm telling you, Lauren, you're gonna be a convert. You will never even think of taking coffee orally anymore!"

I'm sure the folks at my local coffee shop will be thrilled when I ask them to add an ice cube to my Americano.

"Oh really? You've never done that before, Lauren. What's that about?"

"Well, I'm cooling it down so I can pour it up my ass," I'll reply, starting to unbutton my pants. "I'm telling ya—the glow!"

I certainly won't be able to order mochas anymore.

("Would you like whip on that?"

"Yeah, I would, and I know this sounds gross, but could you just squirt it on my asshole? Thank you so much. I don't need a lid.")

But Saranella is just so enthusiastic, I have to try it. She's a commercial actress and she's fucking good at it—you just look at her and you really do want whatever it is she's selling. She exudes this happy, clear, thin-person energy that we all want. And if pouring a pot of coffee up her ass is how she got it, start brewing!

Saranella's theory is that putting it up your bum is more direct—it's sucked right into the bloodstream—which seems reasonable. By the end of the parking lot presentation I'm jumping up and down, clapping my hands with delight, realizing that if the coffee works I may never have to use this old gaping mouth hole thing again.

The fun comes to a screeching halt, however, once she is actually brewing the coffee and setting up the enema area in the bathroom. She's running past Jay and me with arms full of towels and pillows.

He and I have been giggling about the idea all afternoon, making jokes about telling the local police department to be on alert to evacuate the area if something should go horribly wrong. But the sight of her laying out towels on the floor and showing me how to control the amount of coffee flow is starting to disgust him.

They both leave to give me some privacy. I carry my bag of hazelnut coffee in a pink enema bag into the bathroom and do as I was instructed to do.

I clench and hold the pot of coffee inside me, imagining the weight loss, the glow, and the energy and happiness I'm going to have when it's all over. I bet I'll be the only one at the Emmys with that unique glow. Perhaps it will even draw Joan and Melissa Rivers over to ask me for my beauty secret. "Well, Joan, it's no secret. All you need are two things that most Americans have: a colon and some coffee!"

The process starts out peacefully and ends with me screaming and grabbing at the walls, clutching the toilet so I won't fall off.

The period of "Oh my god, I have no bodily control whatsoever" lasts for a good few minutes, during which Jay's Korean housepainter lets himself into the house and is walking around knocking on every closed door, yelling out, "Mr. Jay? Mr. Jay!"

I'm hoping he'll hear the sounds coming from the bathroom and just assume a cement truck is unloading there, but he doesn't. He starts walking toward the bathroom door, which I have not locked and cannot reach from my perch.

"Mr. Jay!"

"HE'S NOT HERE!!" I scream. "Not here!!"

Pause. Now I'm scared I sound so distressed he'll come in to see if I'm okay. Then the footsteps stop.

"Oh. Okay."

Oh, thank god.

"Could you tell him something for me?"

Motherfucker.

"Yes—yes. What?"

"Ummm. Tell him . . . maybe I should write it down. Could I have a piece of paper—"

"JUST TELL ME!"

It is during this moment of tension that I somehow create a bubble. A large gas bubble that causes a cramp that is worse than my constipation has ever been. It starts right then and won't go away until the day after the Emmys.

When my limo pulls up on the day of the ceremony I discover I'm riding with the youngest staff writer, who brought his mother as his Emmy date, and the writer who recently caused a stink by doing a stunt with a local radio show that involved having sex in a pew at a Catholic church. Both of these writers had not been invited to return for the show's next season. I've been officially assigned to limo number "you're fired."

Within five minutes, between the blazing sun and the nerves, I'm sweating. A lot. (Which is not to be confused with my enema glow.) First I notice the large amount of sweat (I nudge the fired writer guy next to me and ask, "Hey! Is that all me? Is any of this you?"), then I notice the smell. A deep, solid smell.

It's not the fired writer next to me. It's the dress. It smells like it's been cut off a dead body. And not the newly dead. A body that was found in the attic eighty years after its demise. The corpse was rotting but the dress was flawless save for its stench. And now I'm encased in it.

Five minutes from the red carpet I realize that this dress has never been dry-cleaned. Or washed. Or spritzed with Febreze. Not since the day I bought it at Goodwill. I did have it steamed when I got to LA. When Jay and I picked it up we thought we kept smelling something in the car, but as always we blamed it on his three dogs. One of them had clearly either taken a shit or rolled around on a skunk. Or both.

How magical. I'm here at the Emmys, smelling like a corpse, cramped with an intestinal air bubble, and missing Mathew. He would tell me that I didn't smell that bad and I didn't have blue eye shadow in my eyebrows. He would say things like, "Even smelling like a dead body, you look gorgeous." And at this point I wouldn't give a shit if he sounded so much like FDR that he was in a wheelchair. Though that would make getting out of the limo tough.

When we arrive I get out of the limo and try to join a group of nonfired people whose limo has just pulled up. But as soon as my foot hits the red carpet this gigantic monster of a security guard yells, "Keep moving! Keep moving! Do not stop! Move!"

I do what I'm told—I don't want no trouble. I start pushing people along the red carpet, urging them, "Come on guys! Hurry up! We have to hurry! Move it!"

When I come to the end of the carpet, I look back and see that everyone is way the hell back at the beginning, walking slowly and enjoying the moment. Nobody has listened to the security guard. Except for me. I've run like I was being chased by a Scientologist with a piping hot pot of coffee in her hands.

Being inside the theater is like reading an issue of *People* magazine and discovering yourself in a photo, standing right behind Tom Hanks. The goody bag they hand me on the way out of the restroom contains lip gloss and a perfume sample. Perfect! I throw half the sample on the dress. But the perfume is no match—the dress wins. I can still smell it. So I dab perfume under my nose. Eventually I'm dabbing it under the noses of whomever I'm speaking with. I keep asking everyone if they can smell me. (The most common answer is, "No, but thanks for asking.")

"If we win, do we walk up on stage using the middle aisle, or should we just take the fastest route?" I ask Carrie. She is seated next to me and has already told me eight times to shut up about my coffee enema and stinky dress.

"If we win, we stay in our seats and look supportive of the folks who get to go on stage. Which doesn't include you."

"We don't get to go on stage?" I say. I'm shocked. That changes everything. "I'm going to the bathroom to get more lip gloss then." As soon as I get to the bathroom I hear over the speakers that we lost.

During the next commercial break most of *The Daily Show* staff comes pouring out of the theater. "Do you guys kind of blame me?" I ask the writers, while dabbing perfume under their noses.

They shoot me irritated looks and walk outside to smoke.

At the HBO party after the ceremony everyone sits around looking disinterested and very soon decides to go back to the hotel.

"You guys are going back already?" I ask. "Don't we all have tickets to another party after this?" But they don't want to go. In fact nobody does except for me and Mary and a few other production assistants. We have the "party shuttle" all to ourselves. At the end of the night I'm in somebody's hotel room, accompanied by a group of die-hard partiers who either are my co-workers or some people I met in the elevator, smoking pot out of an apple and forcing people to smell my dress.

The phone in my hotel room rings, interrupting the warm haze of my post-Emmys morning. It's Mathew.

"Hey! So how was it?"

Before I can answer him I have to finish chewing the half-dissolved Cheeto that is still in my mouth from when I raided the mini bar last night. My pillow is covered in bright orange finger smears. Apparently I couldn't be bothered to wash my hands, or my face, or take off my dress. Or finish chewing the last bite. This is what happens when you can't end the night with sweet, drunken Emmys sex with your husband.

I hadn't wanted Mathew here ruining all my fun. (The fun of coffee enemas gone bad and riding in the fired limo.) But it turns out partying with twenty-two-year-olds and smoking pot out of an apple hasn't made me fun and single. It just made me possibly soon-to-be-single.

I tell him he should have come with me. That we should have made it happen.

"I'm sorry you're not here, Mathew. I'm sorry your fear that 'everything is wrong in the world' doesn't mesh with my version of 'everything is wrong in the world.'" I'm not sure I've said what I mean. I'm still a little drunk. So like a drunk I tell him how sad I am. How sad I've been.

"I bet you looked gorgeous," he says. "And everything is not wrong in the world—you got to see a bunch of famous people, right? Who'd you see?"

For the next twenty minutes, as I finish off the bag of Cheetos, I list every single celebrity that I made smell my dress, and by the time I get to Martin Sheen my dress is off, the Emmys are over, and I am pouring coffee into my mouth. All is right in the universe.

EAGLES ARE SUCH A GOOD SIGN

The moment I arrive at Dini's house for Thanksgiving dinner everyone looks over my shoulder for my husband, Mathew. They're standing up on tiptoes to search behind me, as if he were crouching behind my back.

Normally when people are looking for Mathew I make jokes about his height. I ask for a booster chair for him. Or I raise my hands, cupped tightly together like I'm holding a little bug. "He's in here!" I say, like the Jolly Green Giant. I had a million of them.

But now all I can say to this tribe of married, engaged, pregnant, and "working on a quilt to celebrate their grandparents' sixtieth wedding anniversary" people is, "Mathew's not coming."

"Mathew promised me he'd call me every Thursday at 3:00 during the separation and he has yet to do it," I said to my best friend Gay Jay as we trudged up a steep incline.

Jay and I had recently taken to popping a fat burner ($85 in your local gay-friendly vitamin store) and going on long hikes with his dog Sparkle. (When Jay rescued Sparkle his name was "Sparky," but he changed it. The other dog owners in the park always sit up a little taller when Jay yells "SPARKLE! SPARKLE!" like a demanding chorus line leader.)

"Why would he say that if he's not going to do it?" I asked.

Ahead of me, Jay yelled back, "He can't do it, Lauren! Don't you see? He's never going to 'get down to it' with you. He's never gonna tell you what happened those three days when he disappeared."

My fat burner was failing to burn off the anxiety that had accompanied me ever since Mathew had left. Of all the people on earth, Mathew knew me better than anyone and he had chosen not to be with me. No matter how often I tried to show him what he'd be missing and screamed and cried on the phone, he'd hang up on me and then claim his cell phone had suddenly burst into flames. When I begged him to start couples therapy again, but he told me his only free time would be Sundays from 9:00–9:30 p.m.

He'd moved back home with his family and told me he needed some time to figure out how he could move forward. But I didn't understand what had happened. As much as I'd wanted out and suggested that maybe we weren't meant for each other, as much as I'd never trusted him and never believed he really loved me, the possible end of our marriage came as a complete shock.

"What the fuck happened to 'I will love you for the rest of my life?!?'" I shouted at Jay, who suddenly stopped hiking and grabbed his chest.

"Sorry, I'm listening," he said. "I just thought I was having a heart attack, and I couldn't do that to you. Losing your best friend and your husband all at once—wow. Plus they'd find the fat burners in your purse and blame this on you too."

Jay and his boyfriend, Bryan, consider Dini a part of their extended family. They're the ones who convinced me to join them for Thanksgiving instead of staying home and staring into the fireplace, as I'd done every day for the three months since Mathew and I had separated. They dragged me away from my alternating rituals of watching E!'s *True Hollywood Story* and reading as many biographies about tortured women as I can find. (I prefer those that end with a line like " . . . then she finished her scotch, fell down the steps, and died.")

Jay spent all morning making his case that spending Thanksgiving with a sweet, stable family would make me feel better about my lack of such a thing. Kind of a "so your legs have been amputated, let's go to the track and watch people run" philosophy. (Then we'll go the shoe store and watch people put shoes on their feet.)

At Dini's Thanksgiving extravaganza, the mingling before dinner is easy. I just sit on the couch and watch the back of everyone's heads as they enjoy the video of Dini's wedding from 1983. ("Look at my veil! Oh wait, this is the part where Leslie read from *Winnie the Pooh*. Turn it up!")

Every once in a while the women spontaneously hug and giggle and look around with tears in their eyes in search of their husbands, who are all gathered on the patio smoking cigars.

"Oh gosh, can you see, Lauren?" they ask, realizing they are blocking my view of the screen.

I stare at them and make a little grunting noise. "Ugh."

We reach Dini's husband's vows ("I will love you for the rest of my life. Through the mountains and the valleys. Cuz you can't get to the mountains without going through the valleys. I want to watch you get old . . . ") when I am saved by the call from the kitchen.

"Dinner's ready!"

Jay had a lot of opinions about the demise of my marriage. As he and Bryan and I drove to the movies one night, he shared his views from the front seat while I moped in the back.

Jay's feeling was that I shouldn't act so victimized by Mathew's leaving. I played a part, he argued. His point, with which he was very pleased, was that Mathew loved me so much that he did the one thing he thought that I wanted: He got rid of himself.

"Mathew was probably having the biggest breakdown of his life and all you can think about is yourself," Jay said.

"I'm the one who wanted to move to California so that he could be near his family," I yelled to the front seats. "I'm the one who told him that I wanted to put our marriage before my career."

Jay spun around to face me, thrilled that at least I was no longer comatose, excited that I was back to play with.

"I'm sorry," he said, "but you were like Joan Rivers with that poor man. Remember that joke you told everyone at our housewarming party? 'Who do you have to fuck in this town to get an orgasm? Apparently not Mathew!' Then poor Mathew comes in the house with a picture of you that he wants to show everybody because he is so proud of his beautiful wife!"

"You're being mean," Bryan said.

"How is that mean?" Jay asked.

He continued to scream at me, full volume. But I knew that Jay wasn't being mean, he was just frustrated. He'd been prepared for maybe three or four weeks of sadness and endless repetition of the same story ("And I was the one who wanted to start over again. Make a real commitment to the marriage . . . but then suddenly he was just gone . . . like a bad movie . . . called *My Life* . . . "), but now that we were entering the second month, the novelty was wearing off. He wanted Fun Lauren back. So he kept shaking me like I was a toy whose batteries had died.

We'd been stuck at a red light for what seemed like half an hour when Jay turned to Bryan and me.

"Remember when you were fat in high school? I miss Fat Lauren," he said. "She was more fun. She was jolly. And so easy! You could give her a cookie and she was happy for hours. Is Fat Lauren going to be coming back again?"

I was about to assure him that Fat Lauren would be coming back with a vengeance when I noticed two homeless men pummeling each other back and forth in the deserted Target parking lot—a sight that would have disturbed me greatly in the past.

"Mathew and I never fought. I'd fight but he wouldn't fight back." The homeless man without a shirt had fallen onto his back and was kicking at the air. At nobody. Until his opponent graciously staggered up and stuck his face out to let it be kicked.

The light turned green.

"Oh my god!" Jay screamed from the front. "Call the police! Call 911!"

Mathew just wanted us to be husband and wife and love each other—quietly and without drama. But I couldn't handle that. He was just so "okay" and I was . . . what's the technical term? "Not okay."

"We have a Thanksgiving tradition where we pass a flame around the table," Dini explains to the table full of family, friends, and me. "You light your neighbor's candle, and say what you are grateful for."

She reminds me of a sweet kindergarten teacher, explaining to her beloved children how to "hold the frog when it's your turn." She's talking very slowly and with wide eyes and hand gestures as if for the deaf.

"Oh god" actually slips out of my mouth.

In response Dini puts her arm around me and gives me a little hug. She is all soft corners, no edge at all. Her face glows with so much love and sweetness—or maybe it's some sort of salt scrub—it's painful for me to look at her.

Since she's the hostess, Dini offers to go first. Reaching into her pocket, she pulls out a folded out piece of paper. "Oh my gosh, I'm not kidding, you guys. I had to write them all down!" she says.

"Oh god," I say again, but nobody hears me over the chorus of "That's so Dini!" and laughs and exclamations that have consumed the table.

Dini's family takes in all the animals of the forest. There are Rastafarian boyfriends, crystal meth–addicted cousins, stepmothers and original mothers, commercial actors, beloved gay uncles like Jay and Bryan, and the soon-to-be-divorced who has found herself living with her gay best friend in Los Angeles, even though she did not plan to live with him . . . no, the plan was to live with her husband happily ever after.

The last time I visited Mathew at the bar where he worked in New York, I made sure to have a few drinks before I got there so I could relax enough to drink some more. I also arrived earlier than he was expecting so I could look through the window and catch him getting a blow job behind the bar. Instead I caught him doing something worse.

When I peeked in through the front window of the bar I saw him standing around with a group of his co-workers and regulars, having what looked to be a really good time. He was laughing, and everybody he was talking to was laughing too. He looked relaxed and happy until I walked in the door. When he saw me, his face fell. But he still went through all his "perfect husband" gestures.

"Hey, my beautiful wife," he announced. (Looking caught.) He came out from behind the bar to give me a hug. "I'm so glad you came in," he whispered in my ear.

"Oh yeah? You don't look like you're so glad I'm here," I spit back.

"Lauren, I'm always glad you come in. Don't say that, okay? What can I get you to drink?" He moved back behind the bar with a tired smile on his face.

"I'll have a vodka and tonic, but I don't want you to pay for it," I said. "Man, I don't know what the hell was going on when I walked in, but sorry I broke up the little party. Maybe I should just go." I started to say more but Mathew interrupted.

"You know what? Maybe you should." He took the drink he'd just made for me and threw it out in the sink. "I'll see you at home," he said. Then he turned away and went back to his friends at the end of the bar.

In the five years that I'd been with him, that moment was the harshest that Mathew had ever been to me. And that was it. He wasn't going to play anymore. He was done. I sat at the end of the bar, in total shock. Mathew had been trying to love me for a long time and now he was done.

"I'm grateful to have Lauren here!" Dini begins.

She's kicking off her list of thanks with the saddest situation she knows of, and it's me. I thought there would at least be a "grateful the prostate cancer is in remission" for some uncle somewhere before she got to me.

Dini puts her arm around my shoulders and gives me half a mama hug. "At Thanksgiving, we just love to open our home to strays and—" She stops herself, but not before the entire table feels mortified on her behalf. When Dini realizes what she's done, she leans in and whispers, "Oh Lauren, you are not a stray. I say that little speech every year. Hear me when I tell you, you are *not* a stray."

Just then it hits me that for as long as I've known Jay (about twenty years), he's been known to take in strays of all shapes and sizes—mostly dogs, cats, birds, and fish. He takes them in and they run away or get eaten by coyotes living in the canyon behind his house. The last stray he took in, Chancy, was a seventeen-year-old nearly dead dog that did nothing beyond lie under a tree. Jay would gesture toward him with a sad face and say, "He's dying. But I couldn't let him die alone." I remember thinking that he just loved to be able to tell everyone that he took in a dying dog—it offset his debauchery in the gym locker room.

Now I understand: I am Chancy. Except I'm slightly hairier and in dog years I should be long dead.

"I am grateful for my beautiful family," Dini is saying. She starts to cry with joy.

The therapist that was recommended to Mathew and me held his sessions in his apartment on East 41st Street. His name was Samuel, and he defended every disgusting or disturbing aspect of his practice as his gift to us "in order to keep costs down."

I would have paid twenty dollars more to have him not answer his telephone in the middle of a session. Ten more on top of that for him not to put an entire Entenmann's coffeecake on his lap and pick at it for the entire hour. One hundred and twenty dollars more for him not to say, "These cakes are so moist" in the middle of my talking about my abandonment issues.

"You have severe ADD," he told me. "She must be driving you nuts," he said to Mathew.

Mathew did not respond to his question. He just lit a cigarette. (One reason Mathew agreed to keep coming was that Samuel let him smoke.)

"I'd like to know if that's true, Mathew," I said. "Am I driving you crazy? I wish you'd say that. Tell me to shut the fuck up or—"

The phone rang and Samuel put a finger up to pause me.

"I'm in session," he said into the phone. "Okay. Okay. 2:00 p.m. is fine. Okay. Bye." To me he said, "Where were we? Oh, I want you to read the book *Driven to Distraction,* which will help you to control your ADD."

I sighed loudly.

"What's your problem?" Samuel growled, in his delicate therapist manner.

"Mathew bartends until 6:00 a.m.," I said. "And even on the nights he's not working he's out all night talking to his bartender friends. I feel like he's always trying to get away from me."

"Well, he probably is," Samuel said, stuffing a crumbling piece of cake into his mouth. "Aren't you, Mathew?"

Mathew chose not to answer, which I'd never before realized was actually an option when someone asked you a question.

Someone knocked on Samuel's door.

"Come in!" he yelled at the door. "This is my lunch," he said to us. "I'm hypoglycemic—I have to eat."

A slim young man walked in and handed him a grilled cheese. Samuel explained it would settle his upset stomach.

Mathew and I were there because the only conversations we seemed to have went like this: A said, "You hate me," and B said, "No, I don't. I love you." We took turns playing A and B.

Our quality time meant going out for Manhattans and seeing how long before I melted down and told him I was too fat for my knees. Or that I was so heavy I needed a wheelchair. I'd name and show photos of all the women I thought he should be with—women who I told him were as good-looking as he was. Then I'd ask him if he'd ever thought he was an alcoholic. He'd get insulted and I'd spot an attractive woman whom I'd try to set him up with. We'd end the night with Mathew drunkenly going on about Noam Chomsky as I stared out the bar window, tears streaming down my face, because I was sure—I was convinced—he didn't love me anymore.

I told all of this to Samuel and suddenly he jumped up.

"Time's up!" he announced. "You two could make it but it's gonna take a lot of work. Did I tell you guys how I was John and Yoko's personal assistant for years? I procured young black men for him and young surfer boys for her. That's completely true. I'll see you next week."

Dini is finishing up her list. ("And I'm thankful for our . . . *summer home!* We got it! We close on December 13, so you all must visit. You guys! You have to!")

The flame is making its way toward me at a rapid pace. Everyone is grateful for their beautiful baby and their beautiful husband. I'm going pass out. Where the fuck am I? I'm watching everyone's lips move—watching everyone wink at loved ones, saying, "Grateful for blah blah blah *husband* blah blah blah *baby.*" The flame is passed. "Blah blah blah *husband* blah blah blah *baby.*" It's like a horror film—a scene from *Rosemary's Baby.* Who are these people? What is happening? All the faces are being shot through a fisheye lens, and the only word that I can make out in this secret language of contentedness is *"husband . . . husband . . . husband . . . husband . . . "*

"He's not crossing!"

"He's going back!"

"What's he doing?!"

Mathew and I were screaming at a squirrel that was darting back and forth in the middle of the road in front of our wedding caravan. If the furry rodent didn't make up his mind immediately he'd be hit by three generations of Mathew's family. We'd do the initial killing, then his father would back us up, and his sister and grandma would finish the job.

"STOP! JUST STOP!" I yelled, trying to grab the wheel. The squirrel froze with a look on his face that said, "Fuck it, just go around me!"

Mathew plowed onward with a dazed look on his face. He had had to make so many decisions in the past forty-eight hours he simply couldn't make one more (should he convince his brother to take his medication—just for the weekend—or respect his wishes to not take it and listen to his frequent high-pitched announcements of "I'm losing it, man. I'm losing it," while constantly scratching his face?).

So onward we went, sure that squirrels knew they should move.

Mathew looked in the rearview mirror as I glanced to the side of the road, looking for signs of the squirrel running away.

"Oh my god," Mathew said. He put his hand up to his mouth and bit it. "I hit him," he said through teeth clenched on his own skin.

I turned around to see the squirrel's tail sort of waving in the air. ("Goodbye, you guys! Have a good wedding!")

Mathew looked like he was about to cry. "I've never hit anything in my life," he said. "I killed him. Oh my god."

Tears came to my eyes and I grabbed Mathew's shoulder to comfort him. I couldn't figure out what to say because I was caught up in trying to figure out how to view what just happened as "not necessarily a bad sign." It couldn't have been. It was just ritualistic. Like a sacrifice. Hell, if our backyard were bigger I'd have been sacrificing goats every time I had a job interview. I was determined not to freak out.

If at the next stoplight the car was suddenly covered in baboons—jumping on the hood and licking the windshield—I was going to see it for what it was. Baboons wanting to taste the windshield. Nothing more, nothing less.

Everybody agreed that our wedding was amazing. ("Orcas Island, what a perfect choice! And the ferry ride—so cleansing. And—oh my god—look up! Eagles! Eagles, you guys! That's such a good sign for you two!")

But the big talk of the actual ceremony was how Mathew cried and cried and could barely get his vows out.

I'm in line for the bathroom at the wedding reception when a friend of Mathew's from the bar tells me, "Lauren, the ceremony was the most beautiful I've ever seen. I'm not kidding."

"I know," I said. "I feel so lucky that my friend David could play the Irish music, and I picked out the vows—"

"Mathew could barely get through his vows because he was crying," the bar friend interrupted. "That's when I really lost it. Seeing him cry just tore me up." All the girls in line for the bathroom agreed.

"I cried too," I said. I was trying not to sound defensive as I defended myself.

"Really? It looked more like you were laughing," she said. All the girls in line agreed about that too.

"Wow, everyone's already siding with him," I said. "I can see it's going to be a rocky divorce!" I joked.

The ladies in line all groaned. A few actually yelled out, "No, Lauren!"

I guess nobody likes divorce jokes at weddings.

"I was laughing because I was so happy," I explained. "It was joy." I picked up my dress and cut to the front of the line.

"No, from where I was sitting it seemed more like you were laughing at Mathew for crying," the relentless barmaid said. Everyone agreed that it was "So Lauren!" to do that.

In the bathroom my veil fell in the toilet so I had to rinse it off in the sink. I decided maybe I did laugh. But it wasn't like I was really laughing at Mathew. It just felt so vulnerable up there, with the bouquet forbidding any hand gestures, and Mathew looking so emotional, and in the front row, my mother and my birth mother holding hands and crying. I had to laugh or I would have fainted.

My candle has been lit (by someone's new husband) and is shaking a little in the grip of my trembling hands. My first instinct is to blow it out and sit down. But when I realize everyone is looking at me with sad faces, I feel like I should lighten the mood.

"Uhmmm . . . well. I'm grateful that I dated so many gay men in high school, because now I have a fabulous place to live. Thank you, Jay and Bryan! Though I didn't plan on living there. But it's still fabulous!"

The room gets very quiet and very focused on me. Even the kids—who have been screaming and chasing each other around the table during the other "I'm grateful" speeches—have suddenly gone completely still.

"Uhmmm . . . I'm grateful I'm not pregnant right now!" I say. "That would make everything pretty awkward. So I guess I'm grateful I'm barren! Ha ha!" I hold my candle in the air like it's a champagne glass for a toast. No laughter.

"Well, I don't know that I'm technically barren. Uhmmm, let's see here. Geez. How hard should this be?" I give a weak fake laugh and make a joke that the candle is a microphone. ("Is this thing on?") And then suddenly, I don't know where it came from, maybe it was the power of the flame, or the pain of the hot wax dripping onto my hands, but I start pouring it out:

"I don't know if you all are aware of the situation, but my husband was supposed to be here today. Wait, I should go back a little bit. Mathew and I were going to move to Los Angeles from New York to start our lives all over again. Buy a house. Have a baby. But what he did instead was pack up our car with all our shit and drive off and disappear into the desert for three days. Three days! And nobody had any idea where he was—not me, not his family. He was just gone. And all I had was this voicemail message from him saying, 'Hey, I just wanted to let you know that I do want to see you again, okay? I do.' Isn't that hilarious? It was so formal. Like he didn't even know me! Or like he was trying to convince himself that he wanted to see me again. So I'm calling him and calling him and calling him. Then finally, after *three days*, he answered his cell phone. At which point I started sobbing because I was so relieved that he wasn't dead. And I told him that I needed to hang up so I could calm down—get my breath—so I could actually speak to him. So I hung up, calmed down, and called him back. And when I called him back—THAT CHICKENSHIT MOTHERFUCKER HAD TURNED HIS CELL PHONE OFF!"

I grab the edge of the table to balance myself and notice that my angry breath has taken a toll on not merely the entire table's appetite but my candle too.

"Um, I don't know what the procedure is here," I say, "but my candle blew out."

When Mathew asked me to marry him in front of the Circle K, I screamed "No!" and started running toward the street. That's how much I loved him. I didn't want him to be asking me in some sort of kitschy way. Because the way he said it sounded like he was suggesting something wacky. Like, "Hey, let's wear our shoes on our ears!"

He ran after me yelling, "I'm serious! What are you doing?"

What I was doing was trying to avoid the "Oh my god, Lauren, I thought you knew I was kidding" second part of the conversation. But as I neared the rural street that we'd walked down from his parents' house in the small might-as-well-be-Mexico town in Southern California, a monster truck swerved toward me going about fifty miles per hour. So I turned back and ran to him.

"I mean it," he said. "Let's get married. You're who I want to be with for the rest of my life. Forever."

There it was: that word. Forever. Immediately I saw the twin sisters from *The Shining* joining hands and beckoning me, "Forever . . . and ever . . . and ever."

I hated that word. It was so "and then you're dead." I wanted to believe that Mathew was as good as he seemed. That when he rocked me in his arms and told me I could "relax, just relax," he wasn't just saying that to relax me enough so he could chop my head off and bury it in the backyard. (Or worse, my real fear, that he was saying it just to have conquered another lady—one that didn't want to be conquered by his bartender charm. But he did it. He charmed me.)

Is it really this good? I wondered. Do I really get him? Could I really get the sweet sexy novelist bartender boy? The one that everyone lusted after?

It was like I'd won the husband contest. "He's our prince," his mother kept telling me. "No, he's my prince!" I wanted to say, and push her against the wall and scream, "MINE!"

My parents treated him like royalty too.

"Your dad and I were talking," my mom once said, "and we decided if our family was ever on *Survivor,* Mathew would be the last one we'd vote off."

Then she told me I'd be the first one they voted off because I lied and exaggerated for the sake of a good story. And if she were playing, she'd be playing to win.

The combination of my running and the monster truck stirred up the pit bulls in the yard next to the Circle K. All three of them came tearing toward the way-too-low fence and started attacking the chain link, biting and trying to pull it down. For a second I confused pit bulls with bears and froze, hoping I didn't have my period.

But Mathew was unfazed by what to him was "just a little piece of home" and, using the voice he usually saved for the drunks at his bar, commanded the dogs to "Cut it out!" And they did.

It reminded me of how he always did this thing where he would grab me and throw me over his shoulder and run down the middle of the street, dodging in and out of traffic, with a cigarette dangling out of his mouth. People would be shouting from their car windows ("Is she okay? Do you need help?") and he would just keep running with me bouncing along. My underwear would work itself into a painful wedgie, but I loved it. He made me feel like a light, girly flower. Like I could be his light, girly flower.

"Okay," I answered. "Okay, I'll marry you."

LIVE NAKED GIRL

It's been two months since a tiny Texas psychic told me what I already knew: Mathew and I were over. "He can't do it," she said, her voice sounding like Loretta Lynn's (as played by Sissy Spacek). "It's like you're screaming at a paraplegic to get the phone—he just can't. So leave him alone and move on."

So far, moving on has meant moving into Gay Jay's guestroom, where I've been staying for the past three months. He painted the walls a beautiful Tibetan orange to create a healing space just for me. (At least I thought he did, until his boyfriend told me, "Yeah, Jay said the same thing to our crystal-meth friend who was detoxing here right before you arrived.")

But it doesn't matter, because over the past two months, I've developed my own sort of healing ritual. It goes like this: wake up, look at clock, remember I'm divorced—cry. Today, however, the tears and snot just aren't coming. Maybe I'm sick. Maybe I froze to death.

The soothing color of my room is somewhat offset by the fact that it is always freezing to the point that you can see my breath in here. It's like a scene from *The Exorcist*.

Jay claims he hides the space heater from me because I can't afford to help pay the five-hundred-dollar energy bill. But I've seen the look of "ew" on his face whenever I mention taking a shower while he's home, so I know it has more to do with his wanting to guarantee that I'll be sleeping in a snowsuit and not in the nude.

So I'm under the covers trying to warm my face with my morning breath, and even that isn't bringing the tears. It's so odd. The sadness just seems to be gone, which leaves me wondering, *Now what am I gonna do?* Before the universe can answer "get cancer," I try to look busy. I fluff the pillows and dust off the bedside table.

I decide that the best thing to do is to jump back into another relationship. It's like at Thanksgiving when you think, "Well, I don't feel like throwing up anymore—I guess I'll have some more of that pie."

Within two hours I am on the Internet, signing up on various dating sites. It's the first day of the rest of my life, and oh my goodness, would you look at all the men looking for company. My profile is hilarious. Celebrity I most resemble? "Madonna. From behind." Last book read? *How to Fake a Pregnancy.* I save my only sincere response for the question, *What are you looking for?* "Someone who has his own wonderful life and is happy with it." (I remembered from my dating years that as flattering as it may feel, the last thing you ever want to hear from a date is, "I didn't know I could smile, or feel happiness, or not punch people in the face before I met you.")

The first time someone sends me a response, saying, "You sound kind of interesting. I like your profile. Can I see a picture?" I feel sick and immediately take my profile off all the sites.

Dating is so—queer. So "Oh man, all the good ones are married or gay. Am I right, girls? High five!" But I'd just like to do something that isn't literally queer. Since I'm new to town and crashing at Jay's, every activity I do is gay-centric. Gay coffee, gay gym, gay porno, gay-themed kitchen magnets. It's time for a change. Time to create a new life, away from the gays. Time to get my butthole waxed.

The only problem with this rebirth strategy is that I can't be naked in front of people—even after living in Holland, the most naked-loving country in Western Europe. You can't keep clothes *on* the Dutch people. Of course, if I were tall and thin with uncomplicated nipples, I might be happy to answer my door nude too.

When I first moved to Amsterdam, between the red light district, television, and my roommate, Mauritz, I saw a naked person every three or four hours. If I tried to close the door at a friend's house while using the restroom, I was accused of having something to hide. When I shared this observation at a dinner party, the other guests asked me why I felt I had something so different than what they had. "What?" they'd say. "You think yours is some big party that we wouldn't understand? Guess what, big news, mine's a party too!" Then they'd hand me a stack of photos from their last family vacation where naked Oma and Opa stood with their arms around the naked grandkids.

At the waxing salon they tell me I have to take my pants off. I ask if they could do it some other way, like through my zipper. ("Just do the best you can, I won't expect the little heart to be perfectly shaped.") But they insist on my being half naked.

The Russian woman who is about to transform me from Chewbacca into a lady calls me a "virgin" when she hears I've never done this before, and sharpens her special shears and hedge trimmers. Then she calls in all the assistants and waxers-in-training and folks from the coffee shop across the street. "You're about to learn what you do when something like 'this,'" she says, pointing to my crotch, "comes in to the office and you have not scheduled the extra time."

To distract myself from my nakedness and the ripping out of my pubic hair, I tell the ladies assembled about the time I made a "sexy video" for my now ex-husband, Mathew.

"Oooooh," they all say in unison.

We were going to be apart for about a month, so I braved nakedness and made a video of myself taking my clothes off and "making love" to the camera. Mathew didn't know exactly what was on the tape. I just handed it to him and said, "For your eyes only, know what I mean?" Every time I spoke to him on the phone I'd wait for him to mention the tape, but he never did. We always ended up talking about what the dog had eaten that day. Which did not, thank god, have anything to do with what was on the tape. When I returned home I had to flat out ask him.

"Soooooo, what did you think of the tape?"

"Oh, I haven't had the chance to watch it," he said. "But I'll try to get to it tomorrow."

He could have told me that he and his mom had watched it together and they both agreed I should talk less . . . *anything* but not getting around to it.

When we lived together in Manhattan, Mathew would be making breakfast and I'd shuffle into the kitchen, completely naked, heading toward the shower, which was conveniently located right next to the stove.

He'd give me a quick glance as I heaved my body over the side of the tub, and then he'd go right back to stirring his Cream of Wheat.

"Did you want any of this?" he'd ask.

"No, and I guess after three years of marriage, you don't want any of *this*, either—do you?!" I'd yell back.

"What?"

"Forget it." I said. Apparently, I could walk right by him completely naked and he had no trouble resisting the urge to have sex with me. Given the choice, he would have fucked his Cream of Wheat.

I'd end my shower and walk past him, this time wrapped in a towel, and apologize profusely, "I'm sorry you had to see my naked body before you've had a drink. Sorry I'm disgusting. Sorry, I'm a fatty fatty fatty." I'd continue my rant as I went into the closet/office/second room to dress. "That must suck, always having to see me before I get into the shower, all naked. I know you're not really turned on by my body. No, wait. You said you like my ankles and my waist. Maybe I can have some operation where they make it so my waist went right into my ankles."

When I finally emerged, fully clothed, I kept right on: "Don't worry! It's all over! I'm clothed! Just take it easy! You can digest your food now!"

To which Mathew would respond with a weary, "Lauren, I just want to read the paper."

When I complained to my friends about Mathew's lack of physical attraction to me they would often blame me, citing circumstantial evidence, like how I don't like to be touched. It's true, even a hand on my shoulder causes me to jump. And when anyone tries to hug me they can feel me pushing them away. (If that doesn't keep folks from hugging me, the aggressive and constant patting on the back throughout the whole embrace does the trick.)

After a good day and half spent weighing my options (and nursing my freshly waxed butt), I put my profile back up on all the Internet dating sites. Last night's date was my sixth in two weeks. And it was just as disturbing as the other five. I've been holding my pee for the last hour hoping Jay will leave the house. I'm guessing he wants to leave but just can't make himself without first hearing about how my date went.

I'm just about to pee in my purse when I hear the front door open and close. Except for Jay's screeching lovebird, the house is quiet.

The minute I open my door Jay yells (from the front door, which he's opened and closed in order to get the show started), "Heyyyy!" and comes pattering down the hallway to catch me. The lovebird is on his head, and all three dogs are running right behind him.

"So was he better or worse than Bumpy Tongue?" he asks me as he detangles the bird from his hair.

Bumpy Tongue was Monday night's date, and the guy last night was actually worse. At one point he told me that he and his friends, who are all white tax accountants, like to "talk black" to each other. He said it like it was their hobby. ("Oh you know, I like model trains and talking black . . . ") He referred to Phil, his business partner, as "my nigga."

At one point we were walking on the beach and an African American woman passed us. He whispered, thankfully not loud enough for her to hear it, "What's up, my sistah?"

"Uh-oh," I said, looking at my cell phone, which was turned off.

"Whasssssssup?" Snoop Goober Dogg asked.

"Well, the dogs that I'm taking care of have all been spotted running along the 405 headed toward San Diego." Making up excuses on bad dates felt like the most divorced thing I'd done since standing in line at the courthouse to file my papers.

In the car on the way home I was dry heaving at the thought of all the things I had told him about myself.

There seemed no story too personal, shameful, or damning for me to tell. I told him stories that most people would save for their deathbed. At first the obsessive self-divulging was my form of flirtation. It was "I'll show you mine," only in the form of "I once took my wedding ring off at a party," in the hope that he'd show me his. Also, if I told him the worst thing about me, he'd know what he was getting into.

But once I realized I didn't want to get into anything past the first drink, I kept talking just to keep him from telling crazy stories about his "crew" down at H&R Block. When I got home I sent P. Diddy Taxman an email:

I was just kidding with the story about being pushed out of a moving car by that stand-up comic in Chicago. Bye, Lauren.

Here in Jay's kitchen all I want is a mug to pour my coffee in, but Jay keeps blocking my way.

"So, who were you last night? Were you the sad, grungy, ex-Seattleite divorcée, or the heaving-cleavage Southern California divorcée?" Jay wants to know.

"I was Terre Haute, Indiana, through and through. Are the mugs in the dishwasher?" I ask.

He ignores my question and continues, his voice notching up a bit. "So, how long did it take before you told him you used to be on *The Daily Show?* I think you should make it a personal challenge to see how long you can go without telling people that. I think that would be really interesting, don't you?"

I am not going to bite. I want some coffee. I'm still trying to rinse the bumpy tongue taste out of my mouth from a few nights ago.

Jay has positioned his body right in front of the dish-washer. He wants my daily confessional and until I drop to my knees and admit my sins, I can't get a mug.

"Could you move? I need to get a mug," I say.

Jay's eyebrows are starting to quiver and one of his legs starts to bounce uncontrollably, thumping against the dish-washer. He's like a junkie and I've got his junk—he's getting desperate. He changes tactics.

"What are you doing tonight? Do you wanna come with us to—"

"I have a date tonight with a guy who used to work at the Playboy mansion," I tell him. I'm thinking he'll love that I'm living this sad Internet life. It will make him feel superior, which I think he prefers to me chipping in for the gas bill.

But instead of looking satisfied, he yells, "What are you doing?" and causes all the dogs to start spinning in excited circles and the lovebird to fly off his head back to its cage.

"Dating! I'm dating!" I defend myself.

He reminds me that I've been divorced for a half a second and should try to be alone for a little while.

Taking his advice, I'm alone from 10 a.m. that morning to around 5 p.m. that evening. And he's right, it feels much better. I'm back to my old self just in time for Rick to pick me up.

At the bar, Rick drinks his fifteen-dollar glass of wine in a single gulp, sets the glass down on the bar, and says,

"Whoa, I was thirsty." He re-feathers his hair with his fingers and flicks his bangs back using only his neck muscles. He does it one more time—the feathering fingers, the neck flip. Then he asks me about me.

One thing I immediately like about Rick is that he's got a good sense of humor about the career he had in the '80s—working in the softcore porn industry.

He tells me about a movie he did for the Playboy channel in which he played a judge for a beauty contest. He never had any sex scenes—he mostly just stood in a tuxedo surrounded by topless women and said things like, "Ladies! Ladies! Why, you're *all* beautiful!"

Rick is the most overly buff straight man I've ever seen. He himself comments that many girls think he's gay because "he has zero percent body fat, tucks his shirts in, and has good hair." He works out daily and looks like an action hero, all of which, in my post-divorce haze, is not particularly unattractive.

On my second date with Rick we attend his ex-girlfriend's birthday party. He prefaces the party by explaining, "We call her 'Daisy Von Crazy' and I think you'll see why!"

As we walk toward the bar I notice a group of women wearing jeans so low their tampon strings could get caught in their belts.

"Isn't it amazing and ironic and sad how comfortable everyone has become being physically naked," I say, "but it's getting harder and harder for anyone to be emotionally naked?"

Rick laughs like I've told a joke, then calls out to the group of midriff-baring women, "Hey, you guys!" And they all turn and run in our direction, like in a nightmare, clicking their way toward us in wobbly stilettos, calling out Rick's name, and refusing to look in my direction.

Inside, Daisy Von Crazy is drinking her birthday drink (a Screaming Bloody Orgasm on the Beach) out of a giant straw shaped like a penis and telling us about an audition she's just had to be the naked weather girl on the Playboy channel. I ask if they are hiring any news correspondents, and she gets mad and asks the crew of women around her, "Is she making fun of me? Is she?"

Everybody is so physically exposed, with their miniskirts and push-up-bra tank tops, that trying to talk about anything other than how great their bodies look is impossible. It's like trying to eat dinner while a porno is on.

The deepest conversation I fall into is with Daisy Von Crazy's best friend, Beth. Beth comes right up to me and says, "I like you. Let me tell you something—you're a strong woman. I can tell. I'm a strong woman too. I like you."

"You just think I'm a strong woman because my voice is low and you saw me benching 200 in the bathroom," I say.

Daisy Von Crazy overhears me and yells to Beth, "She's making fun of you!"

But Beth ignores her and leans in close to me. "Listen to me! Strong women have to stick together. I mean, I walk in a room and women hate me. For these right here!" She grabs her fake breasts in her hands and shakes them at me.

"Those?" I say. "They seem perfectly friendly."

"Are you making fun of me?" she asks.

"Absolutely not. Listen, people hate me for this up here," I say, pointing to my head.

Her eyes light up. "Oh my god, I know! And mine is natural!"

Seeing how we're kindred spirits, I try to talk to Beth about my divorce, but I'm interrupted by her screaming in my face.

"Oh yeah, this is my cut!" she shouts, bopping her head to the song the DJ just put on. She grabs my hand and leads me to a tiny dance floor and starts grinding up against me. Soon we're surrounded by men and women, all grinding and groping away. Fake breasts are bouncing off me at all angles, and belly button rings are threatening to snag my full-coverage knit top. Every time an anonymous hand lands on me, I grab it and follow the arm up to see who it belongs to so I can make eye contact and tell them, "NO! No touching!"

At one point a man locks in on me and motions for me to lean in so he can tell me a secret. I put my ear to his mouth and he screams, "Let's see that ass of yours!"

I motion him forward so I can scream back in his ear, "You mean just pull my pants down and show you?"

He raises his eyebrows and very slowly nods his head.

"I WAS KIDDING!" I yell back.

He motions me back in again. "Flip your hair!" he encourages.

I yell that I'm not a prostitute and go to find Rick to ask him if knows that guy. He does and he loves him.

"He's lecherous and stuff, but a really, really sweet guy," he says.

In the car on the way home, I tell Rick how different his group of people is from "my people." He doesn't understand exactly what I mean, so I have to tell him that I don't know anybody else who works in porno. As far as I know.

"They aren't porno people!" he says. "This is just California. It's warmer here, people dress differently." He flashes his capped-teeth smile at me and reaches across the stick shift and grabs my leg, and I let him.

I tell him about what Beth said to me, and he laughs and enjoys my replay of the evening. So much so that he invites me to come over to his place to finish my story. I hate to end an evening mid-anecdote, so I go to his house, finish my story, and have sex with him.

When my friends meet Rick they all say the same thing: "Well, you just got divorced. You deserve to have some fun."

They seem to think our relationship is based on sex, and they seem to be right.

Rick has a giant mirrored headboard where he watches himself flipping his hair and flexing his muscles. And after years of avoiding the sight of my own naked body, even I get into watching myself. My body is thinner, being fed on nothing but white wine and chips and salsa at happy hours. I don't even look like me. In fact that woman in the mirror looks like she's . . . shooting a porno or something.

Meanwhile Rick seems to be falling deeper and deeper for me, saying things like, "The only thing I want for my birthday is to be with you forever." I pretend I don't hear him and ask him to take his shirt off and do some push-ups.

On date nights we do a variety of activities that could have been set up by a TV dating show. We go to batting cages and he teaches me how to swing a bat. We go to video arcades and play shooting games. He takes me to karaoke bars so he can sing "I Think I Love You" to me while I sneak off to the bathroom so he can't keep gesturing toward me and trying to lock eyes.

None of the things we do or places we go are things that I would have ever done on my own or with my friends. It was like I was visiting a different culture.

One night we're sitting at Applebee's and I'm trying to figure out what to eat. "I'll have the deep-fried cheese salad," I joke, but Rick doesn't laugh. Normally he laughs at everything, if only to play it safe and show off his charming smile. But tonight he is chewing his fingers like a wild animal.

"I'll have the appetizer platter," he tells the waiter.

"The appetizer platter is for five to six people," the waiter says. He looks around to see if there's a large group of people heading toward us.

"That's fine," Rick says and hands his menu back.

When the platter arrives Rick picks up a mozzarella stick, takes a bite, and sets it back down.

"It tastes off," he says, pushing the plate of beige food away. He doesn't touch it again.

He's in an odd mood, but I'm just hoping won't affect our sex too much.

At his house, I go to his bed and lie down as per usual and wait for him to put on music. Instead he heads toward the bathroom and stays in there for a good ten minutes. I hear no noises whatsoever. When he re-emerges he looks pale.

"I have an idea," I offer, trying to snap him out of it. "Let's pretend that you're the UPS man and you're coming to deliver a package to me, and I'll answer the door in my robe and . . . we'll see what happens!"

I was amazed by how willing I was to throw caution to the wind with Rick. When Mathew and I were married, I'd once called him at work and told him that the UPS man had come by with a package and that he'd come inside and that we'd started making out. And I went on for about a minute telling Mathew what I thought men loved—fantasy—but Mathew cut me off when I got to the part about "my special package," and he sounded like he was crying.

"What's going on, Lauren?" he'd asked. "I'm at work right now—what are you trying to tell me?"

I told him I was just kidding and then hung up, embarrassed.

But now I had my chance to do it over again with someone who I knew would not only be game, he might also be willing to take a few moments to sew a pair of little brown shorts.

I lead Rick outside his front door and tell him to give me a few moments to put on a robe, and then knock. "Say, 'UPS, Ma'am,' okay?"

He nods weakly and stands outside.

I have to cue him to knock. But he doesn't. So I open the door to find him looking like he's about to pass out. He's gone very pale and his eyes have sunk a bit into his head, like a skeleton.

"What's wrong? Why didn't you knock?" I ask.

Finally he starts talking. "I have herpes and I've had it since I was twenty. I'm almost positive when I'm about to have an outbreak and I know that I haven't had one with you. I know you trusted me, and I have been tested for AIDS and I don't have that. Just the herpes. I should have told you, but I like you so much and—"

That's not sexy.

My robe falls open and I'm somehow unable to wrap it back around me. I'm just standing there exposed in front of an open door, feeling vaguely violent.

I speak quietly and evenly, like a serial killer. "So. You knew that I was having sex for the first time since my divorce, and we agreed that it was 100 percent safe and . . . "

But I couldn't keep talking like that. So I switched to yelling, "I am such an IDIOT!!! What a fucking IDIOT I am!!! I had unprotected sex and—what an IDIOT!"

The next afternoon I'm back at Jay's house, recovering.

"Did you storm out to your car in your robe?" Jay asks, as he shoves popcorn in his mouth like he's at the movies.

"Oh yeah." I say, unable to tell him what had actually happened: Rick started to cry, and I held him and told him all the horrible lies I'd told in my life and all the mayhem I'd caused, and then we slept together again. But this time using four layers of condoms.

"Well, good for you," Jay says. "You see? You're getting so much stronger now that you're divorced—you're looking out for yourself! We're all so proud of you." The dogs and the lovebird nodded their heads in agreement.

Three days later, I break it off with Rick, explaining that we are just too different to be a couple. After all, he has full-blown herpes and mine is probably dormant.

After the dating frenzy and the adventures with STDs, I take a trip to heal myself in nature, alone. I knew of a place in Oregon that required a day of hiking to find, but once there you were rewarded with incredible pools steaming from the center of the earth. Also: lots of naked people peacefully and casually milling about. Before my marriage I'd made the journey with friends but had been too uncomfortable to walk around naked. This time I couldn't wait to be fully exposed and free.

The week before I went to my doctor, who told me that everybody has herpes—everyone has been exposed to it. And unless I'd had an outbreak, I didn't actually have what, according to him, my mother, my sisters, the president, and my sofa cushions had: full-blown herpes.

As I lie on the side of the hot springs listening to it bubble up like a spiritual stew, I feel so free. Just me, naked. Not for a sexy video or a bikini wax or raunchy sex with someone from the softcore porn industry. Just me and the trees, the birds, the clouds, and the hairy hippies—all of us naked as we are meant to be. So this is the feeling all those pro-naked people have been talking about—where you don't feel naked, you feel connected with the earth and therefore connected to life at its most fundamental level.

I feel more deeply relaxed than I have in . . . ever, right up to the moment when a young college student steps on my stomach, lets out a scream, and explains she'd mistaken my naked body for a big white rock.

BORDERLINE

After my divorce, I fielded a variety of invitations for adventure at an array of locales, including video arcades, garage sales, and hotel bathroom stalls. Being polite and not wanting any trouble, I accepted all offers . . . and regretted every one. (The garage sale expedition was especially troubling, since for some reason fellow shoppers assumed I was the one selling all the used medical supplies and kept looking to me for prices, asking, "How much?" as they held a used catheter tube and a Ziploc bag full of gauze in my face.) So when David asked me to drive with him from

LA to Baja, I thought it was the most romantic proposal I'd ever received.

At least until Gay Jay warned me that it was an intense, rugged trip with lonely stretches of beat-up roads, deadly blind curves, and roadblocks that might involve young boys with guns strapped to their legs. "When they stop you to inspect your car," he counseled, "you're gonna have to show a little leg. So shave that shag you've got going or else figure out how to say, 'I'm just a dirty hippie—please don't shoot me,' in Spanish."

Jay also predicted that after the week-long trip, David and I would come back either completely in love, broken up, or dead. "That's the mystical power of Baja. And of brown tequila," he said.

The morning David and I met to load up the car and hit the road, I ran up to him with high-five enthusiasm.

"Baja, Baby!" I shouted, my palm in the air. "Come on, don't leave me hanging!"

"Yeah," he said, still looking inside the trunk. "Could you grab the sack in the kitchen? It's got some snacks for the trip. I got a case of water that should last us the whole time. Are you going to want to stop soon for lunch or could you make it to *blah blah blah blah*?"

I dozed off, so I think I missed the part about using paper towels as napkins.

When I woke up from my catnap, it hit me that I hadn't gone on a trip with a man since I was married. And Mathew and I certainly never got caught up in the boring details of "Do we have snacks?" or "Is there gas in the car?" We usually just jumped in the car and started driving. (Which was exactly what he did when he left me, so maybe that was just "his thing.")

David's passionate attention to the mundane reminded me of the first time we went out—the first time we had gone out since his wife had died and I had been divorced. We had been friends before, but as soon as I got his email saying he and his teenage son, Jack, were moving to Los Angeles, I knew I was in trouble with a capital "T" (and that rhymes with "P" and that stands for premarital sex). We were both single and living in the same city. So when I walked into that coffee shop I suddenly felt shy.

Luckily I didn't have to worry about saying the wrong thing, since David barely let me speak at all. In fact, besides recovering from a sinus surgery, watching movies, and sleeping, I don't think I've ever sat not talking for as long as I did that day. I figured that he was nervous too. Either that or he'd picked up a speed addiction since we'd last seen each other.

The only time he slowed his monologue was when he got a cell phone call from Jack.

"It's Jack, I have to get it," he had said, pounding on all his pockets to find the phone. When he finally pulled it out of his inside coat pocket. It was about the size of a regular telephone receiver. I half-expected to see a curly cord dangling off the end of it. It seemed to be held together with electrical tape.

David noticed me judging his phone and said, "I could only get one new phone on our program, and I wanted Jack to have it. Hold on for one second. Sorry about this, he's home alone."

He directed his attention to the ancient phone.

"Yeah, Buddy, what's up? Okay . . . okay. That sounds fine, but let me talk you through it. Okay. Turn the oven on to "Bake" and then to 450 degrees. Take the pizza out of the box and take the plastic wrapping off. No, that's okay, go ahead and do it right now. Don't worry, take your time."

I couldn't believe I was going to have to sit and listen to him explain every single detail of how to make a frozen pizza.

"The big thing is to be careful when you put the pizza in not to touch the sides of the oven," he said, slowly and calmly.

This must have been what his life had been like for the past five years, ever since he'd had to be both Jack's father and mother. The two of them together every single night at the dinner table. Jack must love him so much.

Nobody had ever given me such sweet oven instructions. In fact, as a kid, when I burned myself taking out my first batch of chocolate chip cookies, my entire family responded to my screams of pain with, "Well, you idiot, did you think the sides of the oven would be cold?"

"Hey, and Buddy," David continued, "if you want, you can put some extra cheese on it. But if you're going to do that, you need to do it now."

I would have just told him to put it in the microwave so as to skip any more instructions, but David wanted Jack to have the best pizza possible. So he explained where the cheese grater was, even tackling the difficult hurdle of figuring out which side made the best shreds (which I couldn't have told him if I'd been standing right beside him, experimenting on the palm of my hand).

As with lengthy pieces of classical music and endless modern dance compositions, once I gave in to David's pizza-making description it started to slow my heart rate and I began to feel the sweet genius of it all.

By the time the oven was preheated I was so in love with both of them it hurt.

After David had stocked the car with water, turkey jerky, and bright red apples to bribe the border patrol police, we took off. The trip across the California-Mexico border was mind-blowing. Every curve in the two-lane highway revealed an entirely new landscape. Every time I'd think, "Now that's the prettiest ocean/cliff/mountain view I've ever seen," the thought was replaced when we rounded the next bend and I'd scream, "No! Scratch that. *This* is the most amazing ocean/cliff/mountain view I've ever seen!"

David uttered a few "wows" and "incredibles!" but for the most part he was completely quiet. Which gave me time to stare at his stunning profile and wonder if the time would ever come when he and I would officially be a couple. I had always been struck by how incredibly, painfully handsome he was—too handsome for me. When I was still married, we'd meet in New York for lunch and I would get high from simply sitting at a table with such an attractive man. I felt a little like a fat mafia guy sitting with his gorgeous blonde, except I didn't have to pay for his boobs to get him to have lunch with me.

Back then I thought if I ever dated David I'd be forced to throw hot oil on his face so I could trust him. But here we were, spending a week in Mexico together, and I still couldn't tell if we were just "friends with benefits" or whether it was serious enough to cover him in third-degree burns.

We had officially crossed the "old friends spending entire days together instead of looking for gainful employment" line into romance one morning two months before at the House of Pies. After our initial awkward coffee date, David and I had discovered we simply loved to talk and talk and talk about ourselves—both of us, endlessly, sometimes at the same time.

In the past, I would have waited until the object of my affection was too drunk to drive home and was forced to sleep on my couch. Then I'd take the opportunity to slur-whisper "ilikeyou" in his ear while he slept and to touch his hair—like a shy date rapist with a little crush. But David and I always spent the early (sober) hours of the day together, so the only liquid courage available was coffee and Tabasco sauce.

As much as I as I loved our talks, my crush on him was causing me physical discomfort. The problem was that I never wanted to leave his side, even though after three pots of coffee, I was ready for my morning constitutional. But I couldn't chance being gone from the table for twenty minutes to take care of business. I was scared that I'd come back to find the waitress in my seat, helping David talk Jack through homemade waffles on speakerphone.

But finally I decided I could no longer suppress my feelings (or my bodily functions). "I need a break from our friendship for a little while because I've developed a crush on you that's making it painful to spend time with you," I said. "Sorry."

"Me too," he said, immediately.

We left the House of Pies and made out in the parking lot.

Two weeks later I told David I was willing to take my profile off the Internet dating sites and stop telling the homeless guy in front of the 7-Eleven that I "loved him too." I wanted to be exclusive.

"Are you saying you want me to be your boyfriend?" he had said. He was sitting on the edge of his bed, putting his shirt back on. He stopped what he was doing, leaving one arm in the sleeve of his T-shirt and one arm out, like a stroke victim waiting for his nurse. Or a widower who was sleeping his way across an ocean of grief to get to dry land. "I don't think I'm ready for that," he concluded.

There was a good chance that he was dating seven other women, so I emailed our mutual friend Martha to ask her why David acted like he was so into me one minute and "feeling pressured" the next. She emailed me back, saying, *That's what all the ladies want to know.* Feeling panicky, I typed, *Is he really dating other women? If he is, he's certainly good at making a gal feel like she's the one.* Martha wrote, *Oh yeah, he's good.* My heart racing, I called her and she assured me she was kidding and said he was probably, as a widower and a single dad, just being cautious.

Which is what I decided to tell myself so I didn't have to think about the alternative. I also decided to back way off. I was falling way too hard for him and he wasn't ready.

When he invited me to Baja I wanted to ask him if he was taking his other ladies on trips that involved planes and exclusive resorts, while I got the two-hundred-dollar road trip with a bargain motel. But I resisted. I knew I shouldn't think of it as anything more than an adventure with an intimate old friend.

In the car with David I wanted to touch him while he drove. Not like how truck drivers touch themselves, but just rest a hand on his shoulder or his knee. But I didn't want to make any needy moves. I decided to pretend we were both gay and posing as each other's partner so as not to ignite the homophobes of Baja—anything to eliminate expectations for the trip.

The first goat we saw on the side of the road—standing in the sand and munching on a tennis shoe stuck to the side of a cactus—sent us screeching to a halt and leaping for our cameras like we were on safari and had spotted a lion.

I should have asked David if I could pee after the goat photo shoot, since I'd had to go for the last four hours. But I didn't know if seeing me crouch behind a cactus and urinate on my shoes was what I wanted for him at such an unclear romantic juncture in our relationship. Plus I knew he had his camera at the ready.

A few hours back, at the military fuck-with-the-gringos checkpoint, we'd been asked to show our passports. I thought I'd spotted some restroom facilities, so I rolled down my window to ask if I could use them, but before I opened my mouth a twelve-year-old armed Mexican border guard made kissing noises at me. Or maybe he was sucking corn out of his teeth. My Spanish wasn't good enough to ask which, so I nixed the bathroom plan altogether, just to be on the safe side.

Fifteen minutes after leaving the goat, I confessed to David that I needed to use the restroom. It was as if I'd screamed, *"Banditos!"* He immediately sped up and started darting his head back and forth, combing the horizon for any signs of a bathroom.

"Okay, we'll find you one!" he said. "Just hold on! It's gonna be okay. Just hold on!"

When he found a gas station, he pulled in and rolled down his window to ask the attendant where the bathroom was. In an attempt to speak the language, he went through his entire Spanish vocabulary as the attendant patiently waited for a complete sentence.

"*Hola. ¿Que pasa? Buenos dias—tardes—dias. Buenos. Yo soy el baño,*" he said.

(I later discovered that he'd basically told the man, "I am the toilet.")

"Over there," the guy answered, in English.

In the bathroom, I held on to the walls like a little princess, so as not to dirty myself by falling into the hole in the ground full of shit. Maybe driving and listening at the same time was hard for David—maybe that was why he'd been so disengaged.

Back in what we called "America," he'd once admitted that multitasking was a challenge for him. We were in the grocery store, and he couldn't pick out crackers *and* answer my questions about whether I seemed particularly self-absorbed that day.

But since we had stopped and my bladder was empty it might be a good time to get the party back on. Remind him of the good feelings that had been flowing between us in the past months—all the laughing we used to do.

"No toilet paper, do you mind?" I asked him, wiping my hands on his sleeve.

He was still so caught up in the emergency of my needing to use the restroom, he missed my attempt at humor. "Was it okay?" he wanted to know.

"If I told you I fell into the shit hole, would you still want to share a bed with me tonight?" I asked. But he didn't hear me. He had already strapped himself back in the car, ready to hit the road again.

"I want to make sure we get to the hotel before it gets dark so I can see the road signs."

I supposed it was conscientious of him. A little boring, but nice.

"*Granny Does a Tranny!*" I blurted out, once we were back on the road.

David swerved and yelled, "Where?!?"

"Favorite porno titles!" I said. "Your turn!"

David had his hand on his heart and looked a little pale. "Lauren, that scared me," he said. "I thought there was something on the road or—"

"*One in the Pink, Two in the Stink!* Go!" I persisted. I started laughing. At least I was entertaining myself.

But David didn't laugh or play.

"You don't think anything is funny!" I complained. He disagreed. According to him, he thought lots of things were funny, he just didn't quite understand what I was saying.

"One in the what, two in the where?"

During the pre–House of Pies stage of our relationship I'd told him about the one-night stand I'd had with a guy that eHarmony.com said was my soul mate. All of my friends—most of whom were actual comedy professionals—loved that story. Of course these were the same people who, when I told them about a friend of mine who died very young in a violent way, burst out laughing. Not because they were evil, but because they were used to laughing at everything. They were easily confused if something was supposed to be *not funny*, and often had to be told, "Put on a sad face. This is actually a sad story."

But the eHarmony story was one that I myself also thought was funny.

"I had a one-night stand with a guy I met on eHarmony and it was kinda hilarious," I had said to David.

The look on his face told me that he did not believe this situation could be hilarious, but I continued.

"According to eHarmony, this guy was my perfect match. You know how that site makes you do hours of psychological profiling to meet your perfect match?"

"No," he said, shaking his head and staring into his coffee cup.

"Well, they do. And I did it, just for fun. And the one perfect match they found for me was this guy who was an ex–child star and our one deep connection was that we both liked 'watching TV'!"

I paused here because this was where people usually liked to laugh.

"Go ahead," David told his coffee cup.

"Oh, okay. So we met for drinks at 11:00 p.m. on a Wednesday night in Hollywood, which is already just so . . . inappropriate!" I laughed this time so if he was feeling unsure he could just copy what I was doing.

He didn't laugh. Nor did he smile. "That is sort of inappropriate," he said.

Jeez, sorry Pastor David, I thought. But knowing every pastor secretly liked a good sex story, I pushed onward.

"We ended up basically fighting all night about gun control. He loved guns. But it was kind of fun to fight—it was flirty-fighty. So we ended the night at his house, making out on his American flag blanket while Kenny Rogers played on the stereo."

At that point David was staring at me with his head cocked to the side, like the RCA dog. He looked concerned. Perhaps worried for my safety.

"I'm okay," I reassured him. Suddenly I felt like I was doing my "share" at a sex addict support group. I considered shutting up.

"Go ahead," David said.

The tone of his voice did not say go ahead. It said, "Please stop."

But I continued because I do what I'm told, and plus the best part of the story was coming up—the part where he was sure to laugh.

"Okay, this is the best part. During sex he tells me to pull his hair. Hard. And I try to but I can't get a grip because he's got so much hair gel in it. So I'm grabbing a handful, then sliding off, wiping my hands on his pillows, and starting again. At one point he grabbed my hair, and I was like, 'No-no-no—'"

God grant me the strength to accept the things I cannot change, I thought, like the look of total discomfort on David's face.

"That's quite a story," he said. "He sounds horrible."

At the time, I thought I could never be with a man who didn't see the humor in the lowest, most shameful moments of my life. But I was trapped in a car with such a man, sliding deeper and deeper down into the heart of Mexico. I felt like I was being kidnapped.

"You didn't even think my eHarmony ex–child star hair-pulling story was funny," I said, continuing our what-is-funny debate. "Everybody loves that one!"

"You know, not everything is funny," David said. He gripped the steering wheel with both hands and pretended to be interested in what the road signs said.

The quiet that filled the car for the next three hours made me want to cry. I realized this was what it was like to be old. You drove in the car and enjoyed the silence. You sat quietly and waited to die.

I was about two seconds away from slapping my hands against the passenger window as cars passed, mouthing, "Help me! Help me!"

The longer I stared out into the desert, the more I felt like I didn't know who I was or what I was doing. I felt like an old lady, asking, "What happened? Where did everything go?" I missed the old drugstore and all my neighborhood friends. There had been no drugstore and I emailed my old neighbors all the time, but suddenly I missed everything. Even the not-so-great things.

My marriage was over—I was officially divorced. And now I was with this person and I had no idea who he was and no one to ask for character references since neither one of us had any friends or extended family in Baja (unless it turned out this was where my ex-husband had disappeared to).

Maybe I was just dehydrated, but suddenly I was overwhelmed with loneliness and started to cry. I turned my head toward the window. David didn't notice my tears because he was focused on a stand by the side of the road.

"Ice cream!" he said excitedly. "I bet they have good stuff." He pulled the car over to get himself a double scoop.

I passed, but added, "Ask if they have tequila flavor."

David, completely sincere, told me he would and took off. I used the moment alone to dry up. Soon he ran back to the car and beat on my window.

"This is the best ice cream I've ever had in my entire life. I'm not kidding! Oh, Lauren, you have to get some!"

With that he returned to eating his ice cream among the families and dogs gathered around the stand. He looked like Bobo the Clown, bouncing and pointing at his ice cream cone every few minutes. The children found him delightful. The adults did too. Apparently they had never seen a gringo so excited about an ice cream cone. I hadn't either.

I wanted a beer, badly. But of course David didn't drink, a fact I had learned way back during that first meeting when we were both newly available.

Noticing the copious amounts of coffee he was consuming, I had said, "Geez, you sucked that down like a twelve-stepper."

"What kind of stepper?" he'd asked, like it was a country-western dance.

"A twelve-stepper," I said. "Alcoholics Anonymous? They're famous for going to meetings and jacking themselves up on coffee because it's the only high they have left, besides nicotine and porno. And gambling. And video games."

I'd kept adding addictions, thinking one would make him laugh, but when I got to diet pills, he interrupted.

"Addiction kills and those meetings save people's lives on a daily basis," he said.

Bobo came bouncing toward the car again and said, "Lauren, if you don't get a cone you will regret this for the rest of your life."

I suspected that wouldn't be the decision I'd regret.

Two hours later, we'd passed a man on the side of the road sitting atop a cooler full of sliced mangos, wearing a cowboy hat adorned with hanging plastic mangos. We'd also passed town after town, which at first glance I'd declare "an adorable abandoned village" only to realize that there were throngs of people competing for groceries inside the tiny cinder-block buildings.

Upon seeing the sign announcing our turnoff, David started yelling.

"Hey! Here we go! All right!"

He was as happy as I'd seen him since the ice cream.

"Look at that! I found it!" he exclaimed, turning into the motel parking lot. Once he'd shut off the engine, he apologized for being so intense during the trip. "I was just worried about missing our turnoff for the motel," he said.

Which meant he'd been searching for that turnoff since we left Los Angeles, eleven hours ago.

Years before, when David's wife was ill, Martha had told me that while Hannah had accepted the fact that she was going to die, the one thing she could never accept was that she was leaving her husband and her son. When I heard that, I'd had the strongest pang—a feeling of, "I'll take them. Give them to me."

In the years immediately following, every time I ran into David I'd remember that pang and wish that I were closer friends with him and Jack. At that point, my thoughts weren't romantic, I simply longed to be a close friend of his. So if he ever felt too sad he could call me and hear about my life and feel better about himself. It was a gift I liked to give many of my beloved friends.

Standing in the motel parking lot, I felt like revealing this to him so he could know how much spending time with him truly meant to me. But it just seemed way too heavy—way too, "The Lord sent me . . . please clear out a drawer. I'm moving in."

The cabins were arranged in a tight semicircle overlooking what was either the ocean or a giant lake (I would have asked David which, but I didn't want to lose his attention to navigational concerns again). A few lights shone from inside the rooms, but it was mostly dark and quiet. The scene was set for either a cute little Mexican getaway or a horror movie. While I tried to decide which, a small dog that had been dyed pink and then gone for a roll in cow manure ran up to us. Soon after, another tiny, mangy dog came yapping forward. Both started sniffing and scratching at our bags.

Jay hadn't warned me that I'd need to practice Spanish for "Get your shit-covered dog out of my purse." The sight of these odd little expatriate dogs—who had clearly come to Baja so they could "let go" and lose themselves to their manure-rolling addictions—made scary Mexican roadblocks seem like a mere fly in the salsa.

Finally the dogs' owner, a large drunk man with a huge taut belly, approached and showed us to our cabin. He, too, looked like he'd escaped America in order to roll around in shit (and tequila), free from America's stereotyping labels, like "mean-abusive drunkard."

Our room looked like an Eastern Bloc hostel, circa 1976. It housed five single beds and nothing on the walls except smears of dirt down by the floor where it appeared the dogs enjoyed scratching their backs. I made a mental note to buy a four-cent sombrero and put it up, for a little splash. The bathroom looked like a jail bathroom—cement bricks and stark lighting and a used bar of soap stuck on the shower floor.

David apologized that it wasn't more posh.

We sat on the edge of one of the five beds in silence, not knowing what to do next. I felt too scared to make conversation. I might have post-traumatic stress disorder from the car ride.

After what seemed like forever, he said, "Lauren, I have to talk to you."

My mind raced with all the things he might be about to tell me. "I've been paid by the reality TV show, *Nobody Loves a Fatty,* to date you, and here's the thing: I fell in love with you despite the odds. But I've already accepted the money for the show and need you to sign a release. Also, I'm gay, which I just realized at the ice cream stand."

Or maybe he was going to confess I just wasn't his type. Years before, when I was still married, he'd told me that he liked Catherine Deneuve types. It had annoyed me at the time, partly because I didn't think it was particularly brave of him to go out on a limb and find the most beautiful woman in the world attractive, but also because it meant I had to take myself off his consideration list. (Which I shouldn't have been on anyway, what with the husband and all.)

Later, when I'd asked him if he'd found his Catherine Deneuve yet, he denied that he'd ever said it.

"What? I'm not a huge Catherine Deneuve fan," he said. "Where did you get that? Actually I don't like her at all." He said it like he was ready to fight about it.

"Geez, you don't have to punch her in the face to prove your point," I said. "I mean, come on, she's a human being, just like you and me—well, more you than me—doing the best she knows how at any given moment. Cut her some slack!"

We both had laughed. And while I was hee-hawing away, I remembered that sometimes I get a double chin when I laugh. So I turned my head to the side and immediately worried about his view of my Bucky Beaver overbite.

"I don't go for Catherine Deneuve types," he continued. "Most of my girlfriends have been mixed race. My wife was half Korean. Mostly I like strong women." He reached those hands of his (which at the time I thought of longingly as "Lauren's future breast warmers") across the table and grabbed my biceps—my guns. He squeezed.

"Wow, yeah," he said. "Look at those arms—you've got great, strong arms."

I worried that he was one of those guys who just went for the arms. I wondered if I should have worn my sleeveless burqa.

"You know, I've always felt like I'm a black lesbian woman trapped in a straight white man's body," he said, after releasing me.

I guess he was trying to let me know that just in case I was a strapping lesbian lady he could still be attracted to me. I'd take what I could get.

But in the Mexican cabin I realized I wanted much more. My heart was pounding and I couldn't get myself to look into David's teary brown eyes.

He started in. "The reason I didn't laugh at the story you told about the Internet hair-pulling guy was because I don't think it's funny. It's hard for me to hear those stories because since the moment I saw you in that coffee shop, I knew that I could fall very much in love with you. And I have."

I couldn't think of any jokes, so I was forced to listen.

"When I hear some of your stories they make me sad," he said. "Like you did things that you maybe didn't want to and are trying to make it into some hilarious anecdote now. But I can imagine that a lot of those situations were not exactly the highlights of your lifetime. I don't know. I just—like I said—I love you."

I couldn't recall anyone ever showing me that kind of concern—not even my therapist, to whom I was paying good money. The trip itself had already been breaking me down and now it felt like my chest had been blasted open. Not in the gory war movie way, but more like a fully exposed, "I feel so close to you . . . oh my god, I've never felt so close to another human being . . . I love you, but where the hell are we?" way.

After standing and hugging for what might have been an hour we left the room in search of burritos.

The restaurant the hotel owner recommended was run by another expatriate—a bloated alcoholic from Oregon. We were the only two customers in the place. He disappeared into the kitchen for long stretches of time, leaving David and me to sit and stare at each other.

I found myself thinking, "Now what? Another relationship?" It seemed so exciting, yet exhausting too. The look on David's face told me that he was perhaps having the exact same fears. I was going to make a joke to lighten the mood ("This will be great until one of us dies or goes crazy and drives off into the desert"), but I was interrupted by the sudden appearance of our swaying waiter, who had salsa stains down the front of his white T-shirt. He asked if we'd like dessert.

My assumption was that David would turn it down, since nothing could possibly beat the ice cream ecstasy from that afternoon. But I was wrong. He started bouncing like Bobo again.

"Yeah! I love the ice cream down here," he said.

"But what if it's not the same kind," I cautioned. "It might be not as good."

I was trying to prepare him—I didn't want him to be disappointed—but David's faith was strong.

"Or it might be even better," he said. He ordered a scoop of tamarind, which the waiter warned was the one flavor that most Americans couldn't handle.

"I want to try it. I'm not scared," David told him.

I reached across the table and grabbed his hand. "Me too," I said, suddenly feeling so swept away by the poetry of love that I was unashamed of likening our relationship to ice cream.

As the waiter walked into the kitchen he yelled over his shoulder, "Maybe you love it, maybe you throw up. You never know."

It was a little grainy, but we didn't throw up. In fact, we declared it Baja's best-kept secret and ordered second scoops.

DIARY OF A
JOURNAL READER

Friday, 9:05 a.m.: I shaved my lady moustache (ladystache) off with Gay Jay's gay razor (it's a gay razor because it's his razor and he's gay), and now I have man-stubble on my upper lip. Then to make it just a tiny bit sexier, I broke out where I shaved. So now I have an acne moustache. I should have left it alone. Like I do with the beard. The Korean ladies at the nail place were right. "You too much hair. You do moustache and arms and chin and back and neck. Please. Too much hair, lady-man."

Sunday, 10:00 a.m.: I keep telling my new sexy boyfriend how disgusting I feel. I give him all the reasons why. It's like when I used to stand and grab big handfuls of fat and show Mathew how gross I was. Then I'd cry and sob in the shower that I was too fat to live. I'd make jokes at parties about how I felt like a giant mattress that my ex would lie on. He'd just lie there on "mama" and I'd flip him over when he got tired of lying on his stomach. I'd also throw in a few jokes about trying to trick him into oral sex by pouring Jameson all over my crotch or getting a giant arrow tattooed on my stomach pointing down. Then we'd go home and I'd stand there—the monstrous mustachioed mattress—shaming him for not having sex with me.

I've learned some very hard lessons from the divorce. But I'm different now. I'm loving David—well. Better than I've ever loved someone before. I don't want to fuck this one up because he is the man of my dreams. I don't want to lose him.

Sunday, 3:45 p.m.: I read David's journal. He keeps this journal of fears and resentments that he writes in all the time. Whenever he grabs that gray notebook and stomps off to the couch I know that he's got some fears and resentments . . . perhaps about the joke I just made about being really good at blow jobs at the gym. I'm always telling him he doesn't get my sense of humor and he's always telling me it would help if my jokes were actually funny, not just ways of telling him how everyone—dogs, women, and children—wants to have sex with me the minute I'm not with him.

Anyway, all I had to do was look at his journal and I would get this huge adrenaline rush because I was sure it was full of entries like, "I have fear I'm gonna keep fucking that girl in my yoga class," or, "I have fear that Lauren will keep getting fatter and I can't break up with her because she'll be devastated to learn that she really is too fat for me," or, "I have fear that I'm dating Lauren because she is like a man and I what I really want is a man."

I was on fire when I opened the journal, all shaky with reading something so personal. But it was a really good thing that I read it—there was something about his ex-girlfriend, and now I know not to fall too much in love with him. I know that he's still in love with someone else so I know not to trust him. That's good. Taking care of the old Laurita.

Monday, 6:30 p.m.: I have this technique where I'll confess to someone how horribly I'm acting and they laugh at what a mess I am and we shake our heads at my antics and it's okay—it becomes just a quirky story. So I told Jay that I read D's journal and he was grossed out. He shamed me. He reminded me how I destroyed my last relationship. Then he berated his boyfriend for not caring enough about him to read his journals.

Wednesday, 12:00 p.m.: I've been taking hits off the journal. That fucking gray journal. My crackpipe. If I'm not feeling right or if I feel off, I open it up and read one quick thing and immediately I'm taken away. It alters me. I act like I suddenly have these amazing insights into him based on what I read in the journal. So, if I read, "I have fear that I don't connect with Lauren very well," I wait a few minutes and then casually tell him, "I feel so connected to you." It's a dream come true: direct access to his thoughts. What he's really thinking. I know when he says, "You look nice tonight," I can run to the journal and read, "I have fear that I keep trying to please women and tell them what they want to hear."

Friday, 11:20 p.m.: We were fighting about something tonight and while he was out of the room I grabbed the pipe for a quick hit. I was hoping to read what I sometimes find—a nice pick-me-up like, "I have fear that I'm not worthy of Lauren." Or better yet, "I have fear that I love Lauren more than she loves me." Something that lets me know I have him right where I want him. But instead I read something like, "I have fear that I will act on my sexual fantasy about . . . " I tried to recover before he came in the room but I didn't have enough time. As soon as I saw him I said, "This is so fucking insane. I don't know how to love anyone. I can't do this."

Saturday, 1:45 p.m.: This morning he wrote, "I have fear that Lauren tries to create drama out of nothing." I keep waiting for the day it says, "I have fear Lauren is reading my journal."

I had a little plastic Barbie journal when I was in third grade where I'd write about what the cats did and what I ate that day. (Nothing has changed.) I remember finding "Jamie was here" written on one of the pages in my neighbor's scratchy handwriting. I was so mad I told his mother on him.

Maybe I should write "Hi, D" on one of the pages. Or, "I have fear that Lauren is psychotic."

Sunday, 3:00 p.m.: Nobody is on your side when you tell them you've been reading your boyfriend's journal. I keep telling different people, hoping that I'll find the one person who will be casual about it. I should go to the prison and tell a child molester.

Tuesday, 1:00 a.m.: I told D I read his journal. It was hilarious! We laughed and laughed. He thought it was cute and grungy and sexy. And then we made love on the torn-out journal pages—the ones that read, "I have fear that I can't handle being in a relationship with Lauren." I wanted to make love on the "I have fear that Lauren is too needy" pages. But I wasn't really in a position to get demanding.

Actually, I was so fucking scared. I figured it was the deal breaker.

Like when my ex-husband peed in the bed and I got so mad I slapped myself in the face. I thought it was going to be the deal breaker. Peeing in the bed is bad, but he was drunk and asleep and dreaming about peeing into a toilet and the next thing he knew . . . But I was awake and sober when I hit myself. It was sexy when Betty Blue ran naked and crazy through the streets and poked her eyes out. But I'm not French. I'm a Hoosier. When Hoosiers hit themselves it looks trashy.

I am thrilled to report the reading of the journal was not a deal breaker. It turns out David is not an easy one to shock. I thought about throwing in a quick uppercut to my chin and maybe shitting my pants just to prove I wasn't going to easily scare him away, but I didn't. He was more concerned about what I read. He wanted to make sure that I didn't have any unanswered questions or hidden resentments that were going to come out during our next Baja trip.

Wednesday, 10:30 a.m.: Now D has seen my "asshole," so to speak. In a fluorescent-lit room. I hate my real self being revealed. I like it better in the first few months of the relationship where I just lie. I never care where we go eat: "I don't care about that kinda stuff. Whatever you're into is fine." I'm just a giant yes-man. My ex-husband thought I loved video games, whiskey, hearing about his exes, and chewing tobacco.

And after I showed him my unbleached asshole, all he said was "You know what, I appreciate you telling me so much because now I feel like you've set the bar for honesty. You telling me this means a lot to me. It makes me trust you more, believe it or not." I believe him.

Wednesday, 10:45 a.m.: But. What if he reads this and starts to wonder why I told him I only read his journal once? (When it fell off the bed in the earthquake. Open to a certain page. I didn't mean to read it, but I was thrown from the bed and my face landed right on it. And in shaking my head side to side as I yelled, "No! No! Not D's private journal!" I accidentally moved my eyes across a few lines.) I'll just explain to him how I'm adopted and wasn't held for the first eight days of my life. And if that doesn't work, I'll tell him what I tell the ladies who wax my moustache: It's hormones.

SMILES, EVERYONE, SMILES

Competition for the room service position at the Pulitzer Hotel in Amsterdam was fierce: portly, twenty-two-year-old American me versus several eighty-year-old retired Belgian men. But somehow I convinced the head of human resources that although I couldn't speak Dutch, I could understand it, and as an added bonus I was able to function without an afternoon nap.

At the end of the interview my potential boss—a big, white, meaty man with red hair and freckles on his lips—asked the standard final question:

"Do you have any questions?"

"No." I said, "Except I'm curious what you meant when you said, 'When the moon laughs a cow's arms get very tired.' Is that a Dutch saying?"

"No," he said, suddenly switching to English when he realized I wasn't quite as fluent as he thought. "I said you must be strong as a cow for this job. With good arms. There is a lot of carrying heavy trays."

The interview concluded as most of my best interviews did—with me thrusting my arm up into my interviewer's face, demanding, "Feel my muscle! Feel it!" He declined.

"That's okay," he said, adding, "I can tell by your neck you're strong," and then offering me the job, explaining that the hotel needed an American on staff to teach the Dutch employees (many of whom had worked in the hotel for more than ten years) how to be fake-happy to the guests.

Thrilled I'd acquired my first full-time real job overseas (which meant I could stay another year in the country), I jumped to my feet and thanked him.

"But don't be fake with me," he said, pointing his finger at my face.

"That wasn't fake, that was—me."

"Okay. But that was fake, right? What you just said?"

"No."

"Was that?"

"Okay, that's enough—" I said, starting to get irritated.

"There we go!" he said. "That's better. Thank you. You got the job."

Right after I started working at the hotel, an Italian hotel chain purchased it. Nobody on staff was happy about this, apparently due to the threat of more Italian tourists coming in. ("Now it will be nothing but sunglasses and espresso all the time," went the general complaint.)

When the new owners posted a notice stating that all employees must attend a customer service workshop, we all thought it was like the Italian classes that had popped up—optional. But then someone wrote "Mandatory" in black marker across the top of the memo.

Apparently, the staff's time-honored practice of yelling "WHAT?!?" whenever a guest tried to ask for help was getting out of hand.

The workshop was led by Regina, a Dutch girl who was more than six feet tall in high heels. She wore her blonde hair in a clean ponytail, pulled as tight as her blue lady suit fit. Her face was the same—tight and clean and blonde. Hitler would have loved her. I liked her okay. Until she spoke—in an American accent that she'd clearly picked up from watching back-to-back episodes of *21 Jump Street*. ("I hope that's cool with everyone," she kept saying. "Alrightythen!")

Regina requested that we all speak in English—just as we should be doing with the guests. She clapped her hands a few times and said, "Cool! Let's get started!" and proceeded to get started with me. "So! Lauren, you're American."

I quickly scanned the crowd of my fellow employees to try to determine who had told her. Who hated me?

"You know this one," she said. "What is the basic rule of customer service?"

"The customer is always right," I said in a tiny voice.

"Say it again, nice and loud!" Regina said, pumping her fist in the air.

"The CUSTOMER IS—" but before I could finish, mass chaos broke out.

The chef, the biggest man on staff and coincidentally, the biggest drunk, let out a booming "BULLSHIT!" For emphasis, he kicked over the chair in front of him, which sent the dishwasher—who had been seated on the chair at the time—onto the floor. But the dishwasher didn't mind. When he hit the floor he already had his fist in the air, echoing, "Bullshit!"

Regina, who had clearly been trained in America and knew how to ignore unpleasant and/or inappropriate emotions, finished my sentence with a smile on her face. "They are always right! That's right!"

The head of housekeeping, with her *Love Boat* '80s-style frosty makeup and frosted hair, screamed as if Gopher had been thrown overboard.

"NO! They are not!! No!"

Regina didn't wait for anyone to calm down. Instead she plowed right along, going so far as to write "Smile!" on the dry-erase board. "A nice, pleasant smile as you walk the halls of the hotel makes you look approachable and gives the hotel a friendly atmosphere. Like that!" She pointed at me, *again*.

Sadly, "smile" had been the personal task I'd given myself that very morning. That and "touch people on the arm when I speak to them." Ever since reading the self-help spiritual masterpiece, *A Return to Love* ("sometimes contrary action is needed—do the one thing that you absolutely don't want to do"), I'd started my days establishing risks I should take to help me find inner peace.

So there I was with a big fake-serene smile on my face that was about to get slapped off by a horde of enraged Dutch people if Regina didn't quit focusing her attention on me.

When she asked for a volunteer for a customer service re-enactment I knew I was doomed, so I prepared to just get it over with. But luckily the frosty housekeeping lady was chosen instead to role-play a scene in which a guest calls on the phone to ask for an extra pillow.

Regina, who was playing the friendliest guest in the world, held a pencil to her ear to represent the phone. The room got very tense. The chef started biting his finger and rocking back and forth in his chair. Most of the housekeeping staff had to look away.

"Good evening! This is Mr. Smith in room 33," Regina said. "How are you tonight?" She nodded toward the house-keeping lady to answer.

"Not good," the housekeeper said. "I'm very busy. What do you want?"

This was exactly what she would have said. It's what any one of the staff would have said. If you didn't actively push the guests away, you'd be accused of leading them on and therefore encouraging them to keep bothering us.

When Regina registered her disapproval with a hurt look, Frosty the Housekeeper started yelling into her pencil. "I'm not going to say, 'I'm grrreat!' if I'm not great. I'm not going to lie. That's insane. You have two pillows in your room. That should be plenty!" She slammed the pencil down.

The workshop ended with everyone filing out of the room donning their creepiest fake smiles to prove that one fake smile could do more harm than good. "Oh, good morning. I am so happy!" they said, like they had risen from the dead. "I am sooo grrreat! Everything is grrreat!"

And it was true—when the mouth said, "I'm happy to see you!" and the eyes said, "I hate you because you are stand-ing in front of me," it was clear that "customer service" was something no customer would want.

I was suddenly embarrassed by what I realized was my over-the-top Midwestern habit of practically screaming, "Good morning" in people's faces. The way I grinned away, you'd think I was interviewing for Disneyland and asking everyone if they'd taken their picture with Mickey yet. It was so thoughtless and needy. After the customer service workshop I decided from that day forward I would be steely with indifference. *A Return to Love,* my big white ass.

Six months later I found myself delivering a smoked salmon plate to Dr. Ruth in the master suite. I wished I were back in America so I could brag about this incredible coup. (I also wished I had remembered to ask her how you tell a guy he's got a faint butt smell that really kills the mood.)

Heart full of wishes, I was on my way to the kitchen when I noticed Jan, the maître d', leaning against the wall with his arms folded. Jan was always in a tuxedo and always tanned. The tuxedo was by order of the hotel and the tan was by order of his doctor, who told Jan it would help combat his depression. When home, Jan spent part of each day lying on a tanning bed that took up his entire dining room.

When I saw him, Jan was directly facing what appeared to be—based on the fact that every one of them wore bright white, brand-new tennis shoes, and were heavily fanny-packed—an American family of six, seated at a round table in the middle of the restaurant. Every member of the family, including the two-year-old, had a hand raised in the air, trying to get Jan's attention.

I could tell Jan was checking out the voluptuous and coiffed mom because he gave a little grunt and his neck was swelling.

Then he leaned the tiniest bit to one side to get a glimpse of the teenage daughter. He was simultaneously taking them in and ignoring them.

"Is that how they dress in Indianananapoli?" he asked me. Jan, like all of my co-workers, couldn't pronounce Indianapolis. Most often they would just sort of "popopoli" through it until they petered out, waiting for the word to end, which it never did.

Soon the father and the teenage girl were up on their feet, trying to get Jan's attention, but also seeking mine.

I tried to remember my new resolve ("What would a serial killer do?"), but like a border collie to sheep, I wanted to guide them. Like a mother's lactating breast to a crying baby, I wanted to provide solace. Like an evangelical Christian to a gay prostitute, I was hopelessly drawn. But mostly, like a Midwestern American girl whose entire moral foundation was based on being polite, I couldn't not help them.

"They probably just want some ketchup," I said. "I'll just go see."

I took one step in the direction of the table when Jan stopped me with a sharp, "No!"

They so clearly needed something. I looked at them, with their outspread guide maps and the entrance stickers from the Van Gogh Museum still stuck to their collars, all vulnerable and dumb-looking. They made me miss my family.

But Jan wouldn't let me help them, under the technicality that I was in room service and it wasn't my jurisdiction. I'd never known him to be a real stickler for the actual rules.

He was more a man of principles, which he quickly made apparent. "First they want an extra fork," he said. "And then a small plate. Then the small plate has something stuck to it so they need a new one. Then the old lady doesn't get her drink and makes like she is so thirsty and starts coughing. It's too much. I'm done with them."

Jan delivered this speech not in a little side whisper in the direction of my ear, but at full volume toward the table.

I wanted to grab the tablecloth from under their plates, magician-style, so as to distract these nice people from the angry foreign man.

"How about a coffee?" Jan asked himself out loud. "Yes, let's go have a nice coffee." He started to walk into the kitchen but paused in front of the swinging door—the same one that earned me a guest role in a Three Stooges movie every time I paused in front of it.

"Do you want a coffee?" he called.

When the staff overcharged the Germans, I was able to keep my mouth shut. When they told the Italians we were closed for renovations, I backed them up. But when they were being cruel to a family of nervous Americans in sneakers and Izod shirts tucked into pleated shorts, my heart was breaking.

As I stood paralyzed, the mother (who looked an awful lot like my Aunt Betty) locked eyes with me and mouthed, "Hello?"

Jan sensed I was touched by these simple people, so he tried a new technique to make sure I didn't interfere with his plan to teach them a lesson: humor. Or, at least, his attempt at what he thought was humor.

"Come on, dum-dum, you big asshole stupid. Coffee time," he said.

Aunt Betty, who knew I was her only hope, abruptly and with a sense of an impending revolution, held a pamphlet in the air and cried, "Anne Frank! The Anne Frank house! Please!"

In that moment, nobody since the Nazis had wanted to find out where Anne Frank lived as badly as she did.

"Please, Jan," I said, knowing the Anne Frank house was just down the street—literally two blocks away.

"No way," Jan said. "They'll just go and block the sidewalk while waiting to get in, and then I will be trying to walk home later and I will be forced to walk in the street and get hit by a car. I'm not telling them. And neither are you. Come on." He grabbed my arm and pulled me toward the kitchen.

He let go right before I got to the door, and when I stopped to try to get one more look at the family, the door swung back and hit me in my face. Clutching my cheek, I ran back to the table—back to Aunt Betty, to Mom and Dad, to my two sisters, and all of our awkward family vacations.

I might not be able to save my own family from the food poisoning that turned Grandma's tongue black in Mexico, or the dog throwing up in my sister's mouth on the road trip to San Antonio, or the gypsy children crawling up my mother's skirt to distract her from being robbed in Rome, but I was determined to make sure that this family had the chance to have the time of their lives with each other at the Anne Frank house.

"Go out the front door and take a right. It's past the church on the same side of the canal as the hotel. Go now because the lines get crazy after 3:00. And be careful not to stand in the street—it makes the Dutch people very angry."

I stood and waited for the family to thank me and ask where I had picked up that American accent. But the woman, who looked a lot less like Aunt Betty up close, shared a bewildered look with her family and then mimicked my voice, using her hand like a little puppet. I don't know what language she was speaking or where they were from, but they all shared a delightful bonding experience imitating what to them was gibberish.

I went out to the hallway to recover and when the family passed me on their way out, the mother gave me what I believe was a sincere "it's all in good fun, have a nice day" smile.

I knew it was wrong, and though I tried to resist, I couldn't help but smile back. "Thank you for coming!" I sang out. "Thank you so much! Have a wonderful day, okay?"

Somewhere across the ocean, the whole Midwest took a break from eating deep-fried cream cheese and smiled.

I'M HUGGING YOU
WITH MY VOICE

H ere it was: the moment I'd been waiting for. Jack, the fourteen-year-old son of my live-in boyfriend, David, had come to me seeking counsel. At last, he considered me a wise adult—someone he could trust for an answer. His question: "How do you spell 'qwef'?"

The fact that he sought me out for guidance on how to spell the word for vaginal fart was an honor. I was truly flattered that he'd asked, especially since I'd been fighting a long, hard battle to get him to respect me.

I wasn't asking for a huge amount of respect. Just enough to prevent him from referring to my Indiana relatives as "doughy white people." Just enough so that when I told him about my jazz musician ex-boyfriend he wouldn't say, "You are such a racist," simply because I mentioned that the guy was black, which, Jack explained, sounded wrong coming out of my "crackery-crack-ass" mouth.

Seeing as how Jack is part Asian and thinking this might be a "teachable moment," I responded by saying, "What if I called you chinky-chink-ass?" To which Jack took offense. Even though, being the adult in the conversation, I pointed out, "That's not fair! You said it first!"

I would appreciate whatever amount of respect would prevent Jack from repeatedly commenting on my drinking habits. Jack's father hasn't had a drink in twenty-one years. I, on the other hand, like me my wine. Both David and I have told Jack it's bad manners to point out another's drinking habits, especially as this forces me to leave the table, slurring, "Listen, I drink! I'm drinky! Okay? Everybody happy? I'm going to go drink with the homeless people in the park, where I'm not judged!" (After which Jack registers his offense at my crackery-crack-ass implication that all homeless people are drunks.)

But now, with "qwef" hanging in the air, Jack was looking to me as a teacher. A mentor! Perhaps even . . . a parental figure. "Jack, I think you mean 'qweef,'" I said. "It's 'q' and then 'weef.' Sound it out."

When I relayed this Hallmark moment to David, it immediately turned into a fight. Not because David didn't want me talking to Jack about vaginas, but because David didn't know what a qweef was. He lashed out at me for bringing up yet another thing that made him look dumb. I tried to tell him, "David, it's a blessing you don't know what it is. A blessing!"

"I actually do know what that is, okay?" he shouted. "But in my day it was called a vart!"

In the early dating days of our relationship, David and I both lived with roommates, which meant we had to put some careful thought into where and when we'd bump uglies. David's roommate was his young and impressionable son. My roommate was gay and had let me know that the thought of my having sex anywhere—much less down the hall—made his acid reflux flair.

Since the repulsed gay man stayed up much later than the susceptible teen, most nights David's place was the default location for the making of the love. But even though Jack went to bed early, one major complication remained: the fact that during sex I would somehow always end up facing the picture of Hannah.

David is a widower. Six years ago he lost his wife, Hannah—Jack's mother—to cancer. She is remembered for her beauty, wisdom, and no-bullshit manner. Her picture in David's bedroom emanated a very strong presence. I could almost hear her saying, "I wanted him to be happy, but not that happy."

When we had sex, every time the "Okay, let's switch positions!" vibe arose I'd scurry to put myself in a position with my head facing away from Hannah. For the first time in my life I could see how being blindfolded would be hot. Eventually I had to ask David to move the picture out of the bedroom.

But pictures of Hannah were all over the house, which wrecked me. Obsessively staring at her photos and attempting to show how okay I was with the whole situation, I would chirp, "This is a nice one. Oh and this one too! Look at her here! I see she's wearing a sweater, so I take it it was winter time?"

Finally, with the blessing of Hannah's family, I moved in with David and Jack. Everything went off without a hitch.

Setting the table for dinner one night I said, "Oh my god, this is one of the ugliest tablecloths I've ever—"

"It was Hannah's," David said.

"Oh. Sorry."

At which point Jack came into the room. "Which tablecloth of Mommy's did Lauren say is ugly?"

Cleaning out a drawer to make space for my candles, I found a dollar bill, which I put in my wallet. Hoping to keep my karma clean, I told David.

"Do you still have it?" he asked.

"Yeah, I still have it," I said. "God, David, freaking out over a dollar is a little pathetic."

"It's just that Hannah's grandma gave it to her when Hannah was a baby. It was her lucky dollar."

Right when I'd be about to break up to avoid any more of these unbearable moments, David would console me by telling me how well he thought I was doing, considering the situation.

"Hannah liked you," he'd say, though I'd only known her briefly many years before. "She loved your honesty."

If only Jack did.

One night, David and Jack and I were sitting in the living room, talking and hanging out. The subject of Hannah came up, and David mentioned that after she died all her college debt was wiped away. To which I replied, "Man, I should tell a few of my credit card companies that I died."

I spent the following hour blabbing a long, pathetic apology, during which Jack stared at the TV on mute.

"Jack, that was just an asshole move—sorry, I shouldn't curse like that—that's inappropriate. And what I said was also really inappropriate and, oh my god! I think I just saw me on VH1! Did you see me?"

I would never attempt to be a surrogate mom to Jack. But during the first few months of the new living situation I tried to think of "things you should do if you're the only adult female in a house with a fourteen-year-old who has lost his mother." One came to me: hug him.

I announced my intentions to David as we were getting ready for bed. "I'm going to hug Jack every night before he goes to bed."

David was touched. "Oh, that's sweet, Lauren."

"Do you think he'll let me?"

"Do it anyway."

That's right, I thought. Do it anyway. He's not the boss of me. Don't let him determine how much love you can give him. He's the child. He needs it. I can give it.

If only I was a hugger.

I'm not a hugger. My mother was not a big hugger. She did hug me—it wasn't like she called me "It" and left me in the cellar to drink my own pee. She just didn't hug a lot. But I do remember one hug in particular.

I'd been busted for stealing a pair of control-top underwear. I wasn't shoplifting—that would have been at least somewhat cooler. I pilfered the panties from the family I was babysitting for, though I'm not sure where I found the time, since I was pretty busy eating myself into a tubby coma. ("Ding Dongs! We never get these! *Munch munch munch.* Dinner rolls! I love dinner rolls! *Munch munch munch.* A bag of brown sugar and a stick of butter! Kids, go to bed!")

When my mother noticed that my butt didn't move anymore when I walked (had she tried, she could have bounced a brick off it), it was all over.

She proceeded to call everyone whose house I'd ever spent time in to check if they had anything that had "gone missing." Then I had to return the girdle to the family and apologize. Not only that, she took me out of school the next day so I could visit the juvenile court system to see what happens to children who steal.

After we watched kid after kid sentenced to juvie, Mom walked me up to the judge. "This is Lauren," she said. "The one I told you about. We don't know what to do. Nothing has helped—we've tried grounding her, giving her anticonvulsants, and sending her to Weight Watchers. Nothing seems to get through to her. But we try to love her anyway."

And *there!* There's the hug.

Hugging Jack every night before bed would be sweet, I decided. I could just see it. He'd go to sleep feeling a little love. And safety. I was going to provide these things for him.

"Goodnight, Dad," Jack yelled from his room.

"Goodnight, Buddy. Say goodnight to Lauren, Jack."

"Goodnight, Lauren."

Here was my chance. "I want to go hug him," I said to David.

"Then go now."

"But he may already be in his bed and I don't want to creep him out . . . Dad's girlfriend approaching him in his bed—"

"Jesus, Lauren. Just go do it if you're gonna do it."

Instead I yelled, "Goodnight, Jack!" But my voice sounded oddly high and fake.

"Why does your voice sound like that?" Jack yelled back.

"I'm hugging you with my voice," I said.

Three months into the relationship, David finally gave me some responsibility in the household beyond putting the napkins on the table. My task: picking up Jack from the airport. My level of pride was in direct proportion to my level of nonchalance.

The morning Jack was to arrive, David went over the flight details. "That's today?" I said. "Oh, that's right." When David called an hour after leaving the house to double-check that I had the time right, I yelled at him. "Come on, David! I mean, come on!"

Two hours later I went to pick up Jack. I got to the airport at the exact time his plane was to arrive. But I went to the wrong airport.

The only thing I could say during the twenty-minute drive from Long Beach to LAX (a drive that normally takes at least forty minutes) was "No, no, no." When I pulled up to the correct airport, Jack was shaking his head.

"You went to the wrong airport!" he yelled.

"Jack, I will give you five dollars not to talk about this anymore today." I said. If there's one thing Jack does respect, it's money, so he obliged.

The five bucks was also hush money for the "Lauren went to the wrong airport, Dad" news. David was on the set, shooting an independent movie, so I couldn't call him anyway. He was *acting* and I didn't want to tell him anything that would affect his performance. I imagined audience members at some future film festival commenting that his character "suddenly became so angry and resentful" in what was supposed to have been the tender love scene.

During his dinner break, David called to make sure everything had gone okay at the airport. I told him Jack's plane had been on time and traffic hadn't been that bad. Right before we hung up I decided to tell him the whole story.

"David—"

"I have to go—they need me now," he said.

I pushed onward. "I went to the Long Beach airport instead of LAX but it's all okay now because—"

"What? Lauren, are you kidding me? Is Jack home—did you get him?"

"No, I just freaked out and went to a bar . . . "

"Lauren, no! No!"

I'd already been telling myself, "No, no!" I didn't need to be told again. When I hung up I was crying.

Jack knocked on my bedroom door and I quickly straightened up. I tried to act like I was sniffling from something cool—like cocaine. Or allergies.

"Did Dad get mad at you?" he asked. I was shocked by how upset he looked on my behalf.

We spent that evening together. He was forced to—I was the provider of the pizza money. We had a very quiet dinner. I couldn't think of what to say. When I did open my mouth to ask Jack how his pizza was, a piece of ham flew out and landed on his arm. I actually said this sentence to myself: *What would an adult do?*

"I'm sorry, Jack," I said, reaching over to flick it off. But before I could he pulled his arm away.

"No, wait," Jack said. "How much will you give me to eat it off my arm?"

He made an even ten for the day.

"So, exactly when did you realize you'd gone to the wrong airport?" David asked, as we got ready for bed that night.

Jack was at the door. "Goodnight, Dad," he said. Then he added, "Goodnight, Lauren," and when he addressed me he used my I'm-hugging-you-with-my-voice voice.

Then he turned around, grabbed his ankles, and farted in our room, shutting the door behind him to trap us with the smell.

It was an odd smell—one I didn't recognize at first. And then it hit me: I know this smell. It's the smell of family.

A FATTY-GAY
CHRISTMAS

This Christmas I am joining my emotional, scruffy boyfriend, David, and his beautiful teenage son, Jack, for their holiday celebration at Big Gay Grandpa's house. I don't know what David and Jack's excuses are for sighing heavily and punching the couch on the day of the birth of our Lord, but I know mine. For me, it's yet another year I'm starting my life completely over. I'm like a foster kid who has been in and out of the system, except that instead of going from family to family, it's fiancé to fiancé.

I've stopped and started so many different Christmas traditions over the years that the only ritual I'm left with is asking, "So what are you guys doing this year? Can I come?" Like a bad animal, as soon as I lick the butter, I'm out. And once again, it seems, I'm up for adoption.

At age thirty-six I still want a home, and I'm ready to prove to David and Jack that I'm a great addition to the holidays. While I can't offer any special Christmas cookies or Famous Holiday Spinach Balls, I do have good cheer. In fact it's all I have, much like Tiny Tim. Except I'm bigger. Less tiny. Thicker, let's say. So I'm a thicker, huskier, more able-bodied version of Tiny Tim.

Jack is sitting on the couch looking sad. I want to boss him around and tell him to help his dad load the gifts, but seeing him look sad on Christmas scares me because I know he must be missing his mom. Hannah died six years ago and I can imagine how hard this makes the holidays for Jack—and throwing Dad's new girlfriend into the mix doesn't make it any easier.

"Jack, Christmas is tough," I say in a hushed "I don't mean to bother you" voice. He jerks his head up and rolls his eyes at me and says, "Moist, moist, moist, moist," because he knows I hate that word. Then he laughs and grabs a stack of twelve CDs to play during the three-minute car ride to Grandpa George's.

In the car, David and I try to talk over the music that is blasting out of the front speakers despite the fact that the only person who wants to hear it is seated in the back. *"THE WU-TANG CLAN AIN'T NOTHING TO FUCK WITH... THE WU-TANG CLAN AIN'T NOTHING TO FUCK WITH."* Normally he would never let Jack play music this loud, but it's Christmas.

"I hope my dad doesn't try to manage everything," David yells.

"If he wants to, let him," I scream in reply. "That can be your Christmas gift to him."

"NOTHING TO FUCK WITH," the rappers carol sweetly.

At a stoplight we pull up next to a car from which the classic "White Christmas" is emanating. David rolls all our windows up so we don't traumatize the family.

In an instant, Jack's head appears between our seats. "The guy who sings that 'White Christmas' song beat up his kids," he says, and proceeds to roll down his window so that Wu-Tang can take revenge on Bing.

We arrive at David's father's house with a car full of wrapped gifts and Wu-Tang still blasting. George is there, waving at us from his front door, wearing a black silk kimono and yelling as we unpack the car. "Merry Christmas!" he sings. "Isn't this weather just wonderful?! Isn't it just to die for? I just can't believe how perfect it is. Make sure you notice the gorgeous poinsettias I set out."

As the nervous newcomer I greet him first, shouting, "Hi George! How are you?"

"Well, I'm *fatty-gay* as always!" he yells back, giggling uproariously.

David cringes and says under his breath, "He's been using that joke forever. He thinks it's funny because it sounds like French for 'fatigued.'"

I think it's a great joke. Luckily George repeats it one more time in case I didn't hear—*"Je suis fatty-gay!"*—and tightens his kimono around his big belly. He is the gayest grandpa I've ever seen and I love him. He not only loves the Royal Family but he knows them. Or rather, he's met them, but he acts like he knows them.

"Does Jack know his grandpa is gay?" I whisper to David as we make our way up the steps to his house.

"Grandpa's gay?" Jack says in mock surprise.

"Wait!" George scolds. "You passed right by the flowers. Go back and look at them."

I do as I'm told and scurry back to see the poinsettias. "Gorgeous!" I say. "Just amazing!" But when I look up everyone has already gone into the house.

"I have to keep the door shut or my girls will get out," George explains. He's referring to his dogs. "Hello, Sweetheart. You're looking lovely." He kisses me on the cheek, with one hand held to the side in case anyone wants to kiss his ring.

"Those poinsettias are gorgeous, George!" I gush.

"They weren't cheap, let me tell you," he says.

"Listen, I'm the only cheap thing that is going to be in this house!" I practically scream—just to show him how excited I am about having a campy Christmas. And to tell him that the best gift David could have gotten me is having a gay dad.

"Tell Lauren that she doesn't have to be gay just because Grandpa is," I hear Jack say to David as they walk into the living room.

Meanwhile, back at the follies, George is saying, "Sweetheart, if the gardener comes around you'll see the definition of cheap! He is truly N.O.K.D.!"

"Okay," I bite. "What does N.O.K.D. stand for?"

He grabs my arm. "Not Our Kind, Dear!"

"I love it!" I yell, just like a drag queen. I'm clapping like I have fake nails on and flipping my wig around and pulling my penis back into my butt to make a vagina. I lean into him—so we can keep our sisterhood tight—"But you don't mean he's Mexican, do you?" I prepare to fling my head back and hoot, but George is silent. He does the polite thing and pretends I didn't say anything.

He continues leading me through his castle and I follow, complimenting whatever my eyes land on. "I love that blue vase. Would you look at how you stacked those magazines!

I love that, and I love that, and I really love that. Dammit, I love everything on *that* side of your face." Soon George leaves me standing in the middle of the living room, alone with my "I love that" Tourette's syndrome, so he can give David instructions for the meal.

During the thirteen years that David and Hannah were married she always cooked with him. They prepared all the meals for all the special occasions, working side by side and feeding thousands. It was their special thing. But I'm not kidding when I say that if someone handed me a red pepper and asked me to wash it I'd have to ask, "Is there anything special I should know before I do?"

Realizing that I'm not going to see David all day since he'll be cooking like an indentured servant, I try to pull him aside for a minute. He asks me not to do so, explaining that he's busy. So I'm forced to follow him around like a nervous little geisha, asking him if he's doing okay and if there's anything I could do to help and whether he's mad at me. But the question I really want answered and finally ask is, "Are you guys going to have a moment to remember Hannah? Like a prayer/remembrance circle or anything?"

"I don't know, Lauren," David says. "Maybe. We didn't make any big plans to. Why? Do you want us not to?"

"Yeah!" I say. "That's right! I'm a monster! If I see you guys join hands I'm gonna scream, 'STOP! STOP REMEMBER-ING HER!' Geez! Come on!" All I wanted was some sort of heads-up. I don't want to be getting high in the bathroom and next thing I know I'm being called to pass a candle.

Usually my insanity serves as a calming lullaby for David. When I start screaming and throwing books at my face he gets so relaxed he could curl up and nap. But right now he has to cook so instead he hugs me and says, "Have a glass of wine. Don't worry. Everyone wants you here. Okay? I'm trying to cook for twelve people. Go talk to my dad." Then he pushes me out of the kitchen.

"Oh, that's nice," I say. "Being pushed away from someone on Christmas. That's a nice holiday feeling. That brings back a lot of great adopted memories of adopted Christmases."

In the living room, George is holding up a '60s family photo of a white plastic tree with nothing but big fluffy pink poofs all over it. "Gee, do you think they suspected anything?" he says and hoots with laughter. We continue the tour past the piano. "Look at this photo of David—isn't he gorgeous? I have friends who grab this picture and say, 'Oh my god, he's gorgeous, who is he?' And I say, 'That's my son. Isn't he gorgeous?' And they just can't believe it."

"That you have a son, or that he's so gorgeous?" I ask.

"Both," George answers.

I spot a picture of David's ex-girlfriend—the one he dated right before me—on the mantel. She is holding Jack on her lap. Their faces are touching. The only time Jack's and my face have touched was . . . never. Suddenly I'm sure what George means is that his son is gorgeous and his grandson is gorgeous and Hannah was gorgeous and I am a troll.

"Come here, Lauren. I have to show you something else."

We pass by Jack, who has turned on the TV and turned himself off. We whiz right by David, who is in the kitchen doing something culinary—I think they call it "chopping." I find it show-offy, so I ignore him.

When we arrive at the pantry, George throws the door open dramatically and says, "I'm worried that we're going to run out of paper towels. What do you think?" He gestures to a stack of about thirty rolls in the cupboard. I start to react, "Oh my—" and he pulls me over to the refrigerator. "Oh, David . . . " he singsongs, still looking at me, "I'm worried that we're not going to have enough olives." He grabs the refrigerator door handle, then pauses—"What do you think?"—and flings open the door to reveal a giant vat of olives taking up a whole shelf. "And I do hope," he says, hurrying over to the dining room door, "that everyone won't mind having just a simple Christmas dinner."

Once again he throws open a door, this time revealing a scene that looks like the roped-off section of a museum. Every setting has an ornate gold plate and bowl for every course. Even the salt has its own gold bowl. There are gold bowls to wash your fingers in. There might as well be little gold servant boys standing next to each chair to wipe our mouths.

My face hurts from maintaining an expression of awe and wonder for every big reveal, but I keep it up. "George, it's unbelievable!" I say, beaming like Miss Alabama. I turn toward the wall, take a few deep breaths to relax my facial muscles, and then I plaster the huge "Oh my god! I love it!" smile back on, whip my head around, and continue.

I thought we had reached the grand finale, but he grabs my arm. "Oh, Lauren, you have to see this." I'm whisked to the study and directed to admire a picture of him and Prince Andrew together. "We just love Prince Andrew," he says. I assume he means the royal "we" but it turns out he means himself and his whippets.

David's brother, sister-in-law, their two daughters, and a few other friends arrive, which means a whole new crop of people to compliment. "I like your shoes! I like your thick hair! I like your . . . ability to let me like you!" I say.

The teenage daughters do the exact same thing Jack did when he came in—they pull their own plugs and shut off. The rest of the adults stand around catching up with each other, I guess since they haven't had a chance to do that since the car ride together.

I feel like an outsider. But I'm supposed to be an insider. I'm here with my family. But it's not my family. I feel guilty even using the word "family" because it might be considered an insult to the original family.

I attempt to keep clinging to Grandpa George, but I get the feeling he's done with me. After we've whooped at all his best fabulous-gay-man lines together, we have to actually have a conversation. I start to tell him how my lesbian friend Karen is in Nigeria shooting a documentary, and he looks at me like I just used very bad manners—like mentioning the poor starving children to the Queen.

I decide to try hanging out with David again. I need my "What are you feeeeeling?" fix. I like to ask him this question every ten minutes or so, and the amazing thing about David is that he always answers—sincerely and for hours, if necessary.

I walk in at the exact moment that David is telling one of the attractive blonde family friends, "I'd have sex with you . . . no problem," in the form of him handing her a butter dish and actually saying, "Oh, thank you. It's like you're anticipating my every move."

I continue right out the other door, making sure David sees me and knows that I've heard him make his indecent proposal. He runs after me and I turn around and wish him a Joyeux Noël by spitting, "Don't touch me! I'm not kidding. Don't fucking touch me."

He grapples with me in the hallway, trying to kiss my cheek. "Lauren, I have to keep cooking!" he says. "Don't be like this!"

"Be like what?" I yell. I pull away, almost knocking over a Ming vase in the process, and go join the other adults who are now talking in hushed tones in the dining room.

Someone is saying, "She was one of the most selfless and giving people I've ever known. Really."

"Hey, are you guys talking about—" I almost say "me" but realizing the joke is not okay, I stop myself. Instead I lower my voice and say, "Hannah?"

They are.

Seeing an opening for family bonding, I continue. "You know, we have this mug that was Hannah's that I refuse to use. David hands it to me sometimes, but I just can't. It's just so her—the style of it, the feel it. Plus I'm so paranoid I might break it. Oh my god, if I broke that mug. When I first moved in I wouldn't even wash it."

Thinking things are getting a little heavy, I change course. "Of course that was a while ago. Now I'm using it to pound nails in the wall!"

The group's eyes turn in unison toward the room where Jack is watching TV.

"Let's keep our voices down," George says.

I want to leave—just walk home. Maybe walk all the way home to Indianapolis, to see my mom and dad and have a *real* Christmas. One where we eat cream cheese stuffed into cream cheese. Where we sit and watch the cats pee on the Christmas tree. My sister will scream at her son, "STOP HITTING

YOURSELF!" and my other sister will fight with me about putting her eight-year-old on Prozac. They will get angry at my big-city, liberal ways and I will refuse to eat salami. Then Mom will get a migraine, and Dad will apologize for loving his new grandson—the one who is hitting himself—more than he ever loved us. And we will forgive him because he's sweet and old now. And, of course, because it's Christmas.

But I'm here. What am I doing here? David and I are a mess. We're not even alike. He's so domestic—I'm a barfly compared to him. He and Hannah had a mature relationship, a marriage, a son. I had a marriage once too, but it was mostly my husband and me hanging out in bars. I can't start all over again with a family that has had so much pain. It will always be heavy and sad and dreary and serious and . . . and then I see the teenage girls sitting on the couch. My potential future step-nieces. I'm so happy to see girls. Girls like to talk and complain. And laugh. And judge. My people.

Both of them are beautiful and young and tough. Their faces are totally impassive—completely stoic and bored. But just because we'll probably never be actual step-relatives doesn't mean I can't reach out.

"Hey, what's going on with you guys?" I ask.

"Okay," Lizzie says. "I want to go down to the basement to look at Grandpa's record collection, but Allison is freaked out by basements."

"Why are you freaked out by basements?" I ask. Which launches Allison into a monologue.

She stares vaguely toward the window the entire time she's talking, as if she's gone blind. "Okay. A good friend of a friend of mine—and this story really is true—okay? Well, she was with her babysitter and they were in the basement. They wanted to play this game—like a board game—but there was this clown statue in the way."

I interrupt. "A clown statue?"

She continues, looking a bit confused by my confusion. "Yeah. A clown statue. So the babysitter called the parents and was like, 'Hey, it's the babysitter—we want to play this game but the clown statue is in the way. Is it okay if we move it?'"

I try to interrupt again, but I can't get my words out because I'm laughing. Allison stares at the wall like an irritated blind teenager and waits for me to stop laughing before she continues.

"Anyway, she said, 'Is it okay if we move it?' and the parents were like, 'Clown statue?!? What clown statue?!? GET OUT OF THE HOUSE!!!' Okay? So it turned out that this homeless midget was living in their basement and he dressed up like a clown so the kids wouldn't be scared. The kids would come up from the basement and be like, 'We were playing with the clown,' and the parents would say, 'Oh, that's nice,' because they thought it was just like an imaginary friend. And whenever an adult would walk by, he'd just freeze—like a statue. That's why I hate basements."

By this point I am laughing so hard I can't physically laugh hard enough. I stand up and walk around to get some oxygen. The teenagers are staring at me like I'm crazy—like they have no idea why I'm laughing, like I'm sick for laughing at the tragic story. Which makes me laugh harder. "What is so funny?" Lizzie asks. "Why are you laughing? It's true!" She's clearly insulted by my lack of sympathy for what her friend's family went through.

Before I can answer, dinner is served. Giddy from the joy that the cousins brought me, I enjoy every bite of the feast served on the Queen's golden dishes.

David is thrilled that I am no longer having an anxiety attack and also that the ham is both salty and appropriately sweet. Gay Grandpa George is thrilled that his son is not only gorgeous but helped him save money on catering. And Jack is thrilled to tell his cousins about a friend who had his stomach pumped after getting food poisoning at the Olive Garden from the eight different kinds of sperm that were discovered in the Alfredo sauce.

Much to the relief of all the cousins present, there were no cream-based sauces on our Christmas table.

As soon as we get in the car I tell David and Jack the clown story, which they eat up like George's gourmet fruitcake (which was thankfully nothing like a fruitcake but more like a rum cake and awfully good). Initially Jack is insulted that we are laughing at his cousins' painful story—he doesn't get why it's so funny. But eventually, after I retell it five or six times, he gets it and he starts giggling so much he even forgets to demand that we put the Wu-Tang Clan back on. We laugh at the idea of the children coming up from the basement telling their parents that they were "playing with the little clown down below," and at the probability of a babysitter checking in with parents before moving a clown statue. We dissect the premise that a homeless little person living in a basement would decide to dress like a clown to appear more like a harmless statue. (*Whatever his survival dictated,* we decide.) We discuss the issue of why midgets, or "little people," are still used as punch lines and how we all hate that cliché, but that somehow, in this case, well, it works.

So at long last I have a cherished Christmas tradition—a precious gift that keeps on giving well beyond the actual holiday:

Jack says, "Clown statue," and David says, "What clown statue?" And I scream, "GET OUT OF THE HOUSE!!!!" Then we do it again until the laughter dies down and I start worrying about where we'll spend Easter.

ABROAD

At some point during the seventh grade I realized my dream of a modeling career was never going to materialize. Models— even plus-sized ones—are required to have a certain grace and relaxed ease shining from their symmetrically pleasing facial features. While my eyes were both the same size, they always seemed uneasy, harboring a perpetual look of, "What the hell is happening?" I couldn't help it—the shock of dealing with other people always registered on my face.

When I first saw the painting *The Scream*, I'd wondered if Edvard Munch had gone to my high school in Indianapolis. The only other kids who shared this look of permanent bewilderment were the foreign-exchange students. Of course their excuse was that they didn't speak the language, but I related to their confused expressions, which seemed to ask, "What am I doing here and what is wrong with these people?"

Though I enjoyed a rich dating life with my fellow Hoosiers—dating the first gay soprano in the history of our high school's show choir, as well as other accomplished closeted homosexuals—I decided to reject all suitors of Midwestern descent.

Instead, I loved every scruffy Lars and pale, frail Henri who came through our school. Dipping their strange brown crackers into Oma's rabbit-bladder soup from ye olde country, they were like magical beings from a magical land called "anywhere but here." They might be butt ugly, with badly cut bangs, but I didn't care. I loved them all.

My fantasy was that in another country a heartier gal like myself would be more appreciated—not just for her fortitude to withstand famine but for her strong thighs, which could help clear the stumps from the field when it was time for planting. In case the Clydesdale needed a break.

In the lunchroom I would try to position myself with my best side—the side of my hair where the perm actually "took"—facing the lonely foreign boys, in order to capture their hearts with my loud laugh and hearty appetite. I interspersed my outbursts with moments of total silence during which I'd grow pensive and stare at the ketchup bottle. Then I'd grab my notebook and start sketching, hoping that this would inspire a foreign friend to grab his sketchbook and sketch me.

"Your beauty is very, how do you say, uhhh, misunderstood?" he would say. "In my country, blue eye shadow worn all the way into the eyebrows is the luxury of movie stars and prostitutes."

The problem with my fantasy was that the host family members guarded the foreign exchange students as if they were brand-new Game Boys.

The one time I tried to get to know the Swedish exchange student, his new American sister told me to not to come any closer because of my perfume. She explained that in his village, perfume was used to kill the rodents and scare away evil spirits and my smell was upsetting him.

By the end of my senior year the closest I'd come to contact with a real, live foreigner was David Bowie's *Let's Dance* album, which I held in my arms like a teddy bear when I slept.

Two years later, I found myself in the European hotbed of the Midwest—the Ellis Island of the Kentuckiana border—Bloomington, Indiana, where I was taking classes at Indiana University.

My friend Emily called to ask if she could give my number to a guy in her directing class who was looking for actresses for his final directing project—an experimental theater scene where I'd be playing the role of a piece of crumpled paper.

Emily and I had both been in community theater productions during high school, and she knew that I'd stepped away from the theater to get a degree in feminist filmmaking while cocktail waitressing at a local sports bar famous for its Thursday night "Best Butt and Legs" contests. The bar was known for hiring only babes, which I found completely offensive until they offered me a job.

"I don't know his last name," Emily said. "Everyone just calls him 'Hans, the guy from Holland.'"

Hans from Holland sounded like exactly whom I'd come to college to meet, meaning someone completely opposite from the guys I'd met in the sports bar, who would ask me things like, "Why does only one of your nipples get hard? Is it inverted?" And the natural follow-up question, "Could you put an M&M in there and then pop it out so my buddy can try to catch it in his mouth?"

When Hans called me, he had a very different question.

"What is your greatest fear?" he asked. "I want you to think about that before our first rehearsal."

Not only did he ask me the best question ever, he asked it with a Dutch accent, which I'd never heard before. It was so unlike how I'd imagined. The predominant influence on his English was the Queen, so he spoke with a very un-American, proper accent, with hints of what I guessed were Dutch influences. T's and th's were pronounced like d's. A Dutch accent sounded like Jeremy Irons with a speech impediment.

Just to ensure he wouldn't fall too in love with me right away, I said the dumbest thing I could have said before we hung up.

"Hey, I just wanted to tell you that I love Van Gogh."

He was patient and instead of telling me he loved Abe Lincoln, he simply corrected my pronunciation. I had no idea that hocking a loogie could ever sound sexy, but when he pronounced "Van Gogh" in its full Dutch glory I fell a little bit in love.

The next day I fell the rest of the way.

From the first moment I saw Hans I felt like I was watching a Bergman film. He was extremely tall (perhaps a medical giant), pale, and thin with wire rim glasses and crooked bottom teeth. He always wore a suit jacket, slacks, and shiny black shoes with a little heel. He had some sort of bronchial trouble and coughed into a handkerchief throughout rehearsals, just like Cathy in *Wuthering Heights*. Dying from TB was just another sexy foreign guy affectation, like wearing an ascot.

During the first attempt to explore my crumpled paper character (which I was told represented a worn-out woman), Hans instructed one of the male actors to stand across the room and tear up a piece of paper. I was to imagine myself as this paper. By the end of the exercise I was in a heap on the floor sobbing. Hans was impressed. He gave me a little nod and then told me to "dry up."

Now I felt like I was not only watching a Bergman movie, I was in one.

At the end of the first rehearsal someone asked Hans if he could leave a message about rehearsal on his answering machine. Hans flipped out.

"I don't have an answering machine, man!" he said in a sarcastic American accent. "I'm not an American, man! Okay? We're number one! Go team! Man!" Then he stormed away, his jacket flapping behind him. I applauded until he whipped around and told me to stop. So I applauded on the inside.

On our first date, Hans took me to his "favorite bakery" for doughnuts. He told me it was a little-known gem that he had discovered on one of his many long bike rides around campus. It was called "7-Eleven."

Not having the heart to tell him the truth, I marveled at the selection.

Hans was a wonderful combination of posh European sensibilities and manners, mixed with a pure goober's delight in American kitsch culture. On campus he had a reputation as "the Nazi director," which offended him to no end, not only because he was insistently "not a German" but also because his parents were of the occupation generation, making Nazi references less jokey, crazy fun for him.

On the other hand, Hans turned many aspects of America that I found offensive into exciting safari adventures. He punctuated every trip to the mall, the grocery store, and the DMV by taking photos and stopping at the customer service desk to find out if there was any point of interest we should be sure not to miss. (This was usually followed by my taking a picture of Hans with whomever was manning the desk.)

He wanted to learn how to drive while he was in America, so I took him out on the backcountry roads of Bloomington. (I taught him how to drive and he taught me how to stop shaving, both of which could have gotten us killed in the state of Indiana.) He'd go twenty miles per hour and scream "whee!" as if he was on a carnival ride.

The first time we consummated our love, Hans used the excuse of "naming all my body parts in Dutch" to dislodge a pubic hair caught in the back of his throat. At least that's what it sounded like he was doing.

He pointed to my eye and made the hocking-a-loogie noise (aka spoke Dutch), then kissed it. It was both nerve-wracking and sexy.

When he excused himself to use the restroom I jumped up to check my back in the mirror to make sure he wouldn't be translating "back acne" upon his return. The skin on my back seemed clear, so I took a running dive into bed. But in midair I noticed there was something in his bed. I tried to switch directions mid-leap to avoid landing on whatever it was, but it was too late. I fell directly onto the bloodstain that covered the sheets.

I begged god to let there be a horse's head at the foot of the bed—anything but the horror of what I knew had happened. I'd gotten my period in his bed—on his childhood sheets, no less. It looked like the little sailboats had weathered a terrible storm.

I'd been getting my period for seven years at that point, yet every single time it took me by surprise. ("Oh my god! I've been shot! No, never mind—I just got my period. Go about your business.")

I ran to the window and checked to see if it opened, planning to jump out and run home and call him when I got there to break up. But it didn't open, and we were on the seventh floor.

I ripped the sheets off the bed and started shoving them underneath it. But there were books under the bed taking up valuable soiled-sheet room. I tried cramming the sheets in my purse, but they wouldn't fit there either.

When Hans returned I was forcing the sheets into his desk drawer.

"What are you doing?" he asked. He immediately grabbed at his sheets, which started a tug of war until I lost my grip, weakened by blood loss and shame.

"What is this?" he asked, noticing the blood. He looked down at his bare stomach, as if checking to see if it was coming from him.

Maybe there was some program like witness protection where girls who have done this are given money to move to new towns and get plastic surgery and new identities.

"Hans, I'm so sorry," I said. "It's me."

When it dawned on him what had happened, Hans unfurled the sheets and held them out in front of him.

"Look at that!" he exclaimed. "Look!"

I was looking. Was he trying to shame me? What was he going to do next—wipe my nose in it?

But he was smiling. And then he was laughing—big, open-mouthed, booming laughter.

"Yeah, man!" he said. "I love it!" He started hugging the sheets.

"Oh, don't do that, Hans," I said.

"I've been with a real woman and I've got the evidence right here!" he continued. "All right! I can't wait to do laundry tomorrow!"

He couldn't wait to show the other boys in his dorm. At one point he was so excited that I worried he was going to get out his camera.

The last time I'd heard a man even acknowledge the fact that women have periods was when one of the cooks at the sports bar told me that he didn't trust anything that bleeds for five days and doesn't die.

I loved Hans and all of his people. I loved how you couldn't gross out the Dutch. Except by mistaking them for Germans.

Since things were going so well, we planned a summer trip to Amsterdam to meet his parents. In preparation, Hans started teaching me a few simple Dutch sentences. He began with the essentials that every traveler abroad should learn, like, "Your son has a very large penis." To avoid any awkward silences when I met his mother.

Upon arrival in Hans's hometown, I was greeted like the Allied troops. His entire family—mother, father, sister, brother, and grandpa—all clumped together in front of their modest village home waving little American flags and singing the theme song from *The Mickey Mouse Club*.

His mother took the lead vocal part as the other members of the family backed her by mumbling the basic tune, but without using any actual English words.

"Who the leader in the club she is you and me!" his mother sang, as I stood five feet in front of them clutching Hans's arm.

When it got to the point where his mother was simply chanting "Mickey! Mickey! Mickey!" over and over again, I realized that nobody—not even I—knew exactly how the song ended. It just petered out as Hans's younger brother (who looked like an angry Muppet version of Hans) tried to spell the letters "M-i-c-k-e-y" and couldn't. He took this failure very hard. He stomped his foot on the ground after getting stuck on the letter "e" and then shoved his hands in his pockets and glared at me for causing all this pain.

Hans's mom saved the moment by jumping forward, yanking Hans from me, and giving her son—whom she'd not seen in seven months—and then me Dutch kisses.

"Hello, Lauren!" she said. "We love you!"

Everybody laughed.

"Thank you!" I yelled. "I love your son! He's so tall!" I mimed "so tall" by acting as if a giant was coming toward me and was going to step on me. I even gave a little scream: "Ahh! Don't step on me!"

The flags stopped waving.

"You are adopted?" Hans's mother asked.

Hans said something to her in Dutch, which made his Muppet brother even madder, and they started hocking and barking at one another.

"It's okay," I said. "I'm adopted. It's no big deal. Everybody stay calm," I said.

I found out later that Hans's family had decided the reason that I'd so easily left my family and come to Europe for the summer was because I was adopted and didn't have a real family.

While the rest of the family babbled away to Hans, his brother glared at me. When I tried to tell him I was struck by how different everything looked—how much greener the grass was, how much cleaner the streets were—he cut me off.

"Hans is my brother!" he shouted, as if we were in the middle of a fight. Then he walked away and joined the rest of his family, who were waiting to see what Hans had brought him from Indiana.

This was about the point when I started shaking. The sound of the entire family barking away in Dutch, interspersing my name in an unpleasant tone, was making me anxious.

I went to the bathroom to collect myself, but I couldn't figure out how to flush the toilet. There was no water in the bowl—it was just an empty toilet, which meant using it was like going to the bathroom on a plate. Finally I used handfuls of water from the little sink by the toilet to rinse away my business.

When I emerged, Hans's family was setting the table for dinner. Here was my chance to experience exotic food in a foreign land. Bring on the rabbit-bladder soup and brown crackers! I was eager to try whatever "we use every part of the animal" old-country recipe they threw at me. I just hoped to god that I didn't eat too much or too little.

But when Grandpa started yelling and pointing at my bread, I knew that I'd done one or the other.

I balanced my slice of white bread with peanut butter in one hand as a fight like I'd never witnessed broke out at the dining room table. There was throwing of silverware. Shouting and pounding on the table. At one point Hans's mother stood up and started opening and banging shut all the cabinets in the kitchen. And every other word seemed to be "Lauren."

"Bark-bark-LAUREN! Bark-hocker-bark-AMERICAN-hocker-LAUREN-bark-bark!"

I kept trying to grab Hans's sleeve to ask him what was going on, but he was completely engrossed in the fight. Ever since we'd landed he'd seemed like a different, more agitated person. When I finally excused myself from the table so I could go cry in the bathroom, he noticed how upset I was and filled me in on what the hubbub was about.

"My father thinks you use too much peanut butter on your bread," he said, pointing to my very modest spreading of peanut butter. In Indiana, this would've been considered nothing. It was the peanut butter smearing of an anorexic.

"Ja!" Hans's father said. "Too much." He picked up the jar to show how light and empty it now felt.

As the family watched in silence, I scraped all of the peanut butter off my bread and wiped it back into the jar. Once my bread was bare the family settled down and enjoyed the rest of their meal.

At the end of my first day in Europe, Hans tucked me into a little bed next to his in the attic. He announced that we wouldn't be staying long at his parents' house because his brother didn't like me and had told Hans to get rid of me.

We ended up finding not just a place of our own for the summer but a houseboat—an adorable little floating one-room apartment that was a twenty-minute bike ride from the center of Amsterdam.

Whenever I was asked by his Dutch friends, who spoke very clear English, "What is your name?" I'd just stare at Hans, waiting for him to answer this complicated question on my behalf. Hans needed some time when I wasn't clinging to his leg in complete terror of saying the wrong thing, taking the wrong turn, or using too much peanut butter.

So one day he decided to leave me all alone on the houseboat for a few hours while he went to meet some old school friends at a cafe.

As he rode away on his bike, I sat by the window preparing to stay there all day waiting for him to get home. Moments later, two white swans swam right up to the window and looked in at me. Assuming they'd escaped from the zoo, I jumped up and ran outside to tell someone to call the authorities and let them know we'd found them.

The swans were the most exotic animals I'd ever seen. I looked around to see if there was an elephant and a flamingo heading my way too—perhaps a circus truck had crashed on the road or there was a fire at the zoo. Who knows, but something incredible was happening.

An old Dutch guy was washing his boat and for the first time since I'd arrived, I lost my shyness and called to him.

"Look! Look!" I shouted, pointing at the swans.

He smiled and nodded his head, assuming I was mentally handicapped. He pointed to the clouds and tried to get me excited about them too.

I couldn't wait to tell Hans what I'd seen. But when he finally got home, he patted my head, gave me a cookie, and told me that swans were as common as pigeons but a lot meaner, so stay away from them.

The next day I announced I was going to go into Amsterdam by myself, for the first time. To prove to Hans that I was still the brave, independent girl he'd fallen in love with.

The route was fairly simple—just go over the bridge, ride along the park, and follow the street where the trams ran to the city center.

As I rode by the park trying to look casual and Dutch, a man with his pants down around his ankles jumped out of the bushes and started masturbating in my direction. He was yelling something in Dutch that I assumed was, "I kill you, I kill you!" (Pause to adjust grip.) "I kill you!"

I started peddling wildly and was about to yell for someone to call the police when I noticed a group of Dutch mothers pushing their strollers nearby. The man was still masturbating and yelling in full view of the mothers, but either what he was saying was hilarious or he was a beloved park fixture (Old Crazy Wacking Peter!), because the group of young women just looked at each other and laughed.

When I neared the city center I was hoping to find the famous flower market. I thought I could offset being masturbated at with a nice bouquet of tulips. Instead I ended up in the wacking capital of Europe, the red light district.

Back in Indiana, Hans and I had both joked about the red light district, and I'd told him how I couldn't wait to finally experience a culture that was not so puritanical—one that loved and fostered its prostitutes. Now that I found myself in the middle of it, I turned into a Baptist housewife.

Every prostitute dressed in fluorescent lingerie and tapping at the window she stood at caused me to clutch my map of Amsterdam like a bible. When I stopped to consult my map and find out how to get out of there, I was relieved to discover that I was in front of some sort of drugstore with a display in the window featuring various crackers and jams. They also had a TV set playing a grainy video of what looked like one my childhood favorites, *Old Yeller*.

I didn't remember the shot of Old Yeller running in slow motion through a field of grass, so I put down my map and got caught up in what I thought was a part of the movie I'd forgotten. Or maybe it was a European version of the classic. But when Old Yeller reached a naked lady laying on her back with her legs spread wide open, I screamed.

Overwhelmed, I dismounted my bike at the city park and sat in the grass until I got my heart rate down.

I had pulled my journal out in an attempt at calming myself down, when a man sat down right next to me. I looked around to see if perhaps Vondelpark had been suddenly swarmed with people, leaving the spot next to me as the only place to sit. It wasn't. I was surrounded by nothing but empty, green fields.

The man's breathing sounded disturbed and erratic. Then I saw his shaking hands as he pulled out a porno magazine and showed me one of the pictures.

"Do you like zees?" he asked in a German accent.

I screamed at him. "No, I don't like them!" Maybe if he moved his thumb so I could see what the woman was doing to the other woman I might be interested, but I continued yelling.

"No! I don't like that! This is a park! A peaceful park!"

By the time I got to the part about "how dare he disturb my journaling" he was gone, leaving me screaming at no one. Just like the junkies I'd been seeing all day.

Amsterdam had shocked me into a state of nervous grannyhood. Ever since I arrived at Schiphol Airport, I felt like a completely different person. Not the free-spirited, fun young girl living her European dream I'd imagined I'd be, but more of a traumatized shell of person with no sense of self.

After so many years spent longing to experience something foreign and fantasizing that I'd feel more at home once I actually left my home, I had no idea who I was.

I had always fancied myself a progressive, liberal, artsy hippie girl trapped in the conservative Midwest and not easily shocked—in fact, I did the shocking back home. But from the first day I arrived, I felt like a scared, prudish, jumpy, overly polite American girl.

Hans's idea to help calm my culture shock was to mix me in with his school friends. The old gang consisted of about seven young Dutch men and women who had all lusted after and dated and broken up with each other four or five times since they were in kindergarten together. The leader of the group was Rini, a busty, proud, stoic, blonde bombshell who greeted me at her door with traditional Dutch kisses on the cheeks.

"Wow," she said. "You have so much makeup on. Are you going to the prom tonight?"

Her old friends applauded her clever cultural reference. I tried to let everyone know that it was just lipstick—I'd only put on lipstick, I swore—but they only laughed at my panic. "So American!" they all agreed.

But the group was welcoming and polite, speaking English throughout the night so I wouldn't feel excluded. I did feel more like a part of the group, until dinner was over and the subject of America came up.

"I would *not* want to grow old in America," someone said.

From there it took off.

"Well, I'd rather be old than gay in America," someone else argued.

"I'd rather be gay than a young black man."

"I'd rather be a young black man than a young black woman!"

"I'd rather be a young black woman than a young black lesbian woman."

"I'd rather be a Vietnam vet than a crack baby."

"I'd rather be a crack baby than a Native American!"

"And I'd rather be a Native American than a homeless gay farmer!" I finally said, adding, "Am I the only one who's waiting for that lid to come off that old cookie tin?"

That got me my first laugh since arriving in Amsterdam, from everybody but Hans. He was looking irritated, which was why I took Rini up on her offer to help with the dishes.

"So what made you fall in love with my Hans?" she asked, as soon as we got to the kitchen.

"He's not yours, he's mine!" I answered, totally kidding.

"You can have him," she replied, completely seriously.

"Hans is not like the other Dutch men," she told me. "He's quite different. He's never quite fit in. But overseas he's had much more success. Dutch women want nothing to do with him, but the foreign girls seem to really like him."

"Yeah, those of us from the desperate troll countries love him," I almost said. But I decided to take a chance and actually try to talk with her. I needed a girlfriend, and though I might have preferred an uglier, fatter one, this might be my only choice. I launched in:

"You put a guy back among his own people and it's just very different. In Indiana it was like we were living this long romantic scene out of a foreign movie. But since we've been here, things have changed. And you know, back home I really fancied myself this radical, liberal hippie girl. I thought everyone else was so prudish and uptight. And now it's me. And Hans—oh my god!—he fights with everyone here! He gets mad if he thinks people cut in front of him at the grocery store. In Indiana he was too busy laughing at all the different kinds of gum to care. I think we're both freaking out a bit."

I stopped talking even though I could have gone on and on. It had been so long since I'd actually been able to articulate anything besides, "Brown bread, please. Sliced, please. Thank you, please."

Rini turned off the water and let out a little laugh. "Wow, you talk *very* fast," she said, and walked out of the kitchen.

A month later Hans asked Rini to have sex with him after a night of beers and meatballs at their old hangout, The Mole Hole. She called me the next day and turned him in.

"I told him no," she said, and hung up.

I was supposed to return to America in two weeks, which was two weeks too long to spend in the company of a wannabe cheater.

I announced to Hans that I was breaking up with him and going to live with a friend that Rini had kindly set me up with—an art student who was willing to trade rent for my posing naked holding a giant metal pole in my hands for three hours a day.

Hans went into a rage and tried to tear his turtleneck off. As he pulled at it, the stitching gave way at the neck and left him on the floor with only the cloth around his neck. He looked like a crazed priest.

As I was on the steps of the houseboat with my bags packed, screaming and crying for him to let me go, I realized I finally had the emotional references I needed a year ago to play what had then seemed like a foreign role—the "crumpled paper." The irony was that since we were breaking up, he'd never cast me in that role again.

As I rode away on my bike, Hans screamed after me that he loved me. When I didn't respond, he screamed that he hated me. It was all very Bergmanesque.

On the day I was to return home I sat in a cafe and stared at my return ticket.

Though I'd been there three months, Amsterdam still seemed completely foreign and intense, which made me want to get out. Take a break. Be able to buy a stamp without having to prepare days ahead of time and recover for hours afterward.

But if I went home now, I'd be returning as the exact same person I was when I first arrived (except I'd learned how to flush the toilets and hop off my bike while it was still moving without toppling into a pile of rottweiler shit). I'd also be going home single, and I knew the foreign boy dating pool was much larger in Holland than in Indiana.

If I didn't start packing within the hour I wouldn't make the plane. And if I didn't make the plane I didn't know what would happen. I had no idea where I'd live, what I'd do for money, or how I'd ever manage to get back home. But it seemed sad to abandon the adrenaline rush of navigating each day from scratch in exchange for the calm of the known.

I decided to stay—it was too life-threatening not to. Plus, trying to figure out how to tell the clerk at the train station I needed a "one-way ticket to the airport" would take me at least an hour. And I'd just ordered myself a cheese sandwich and didn't want to feel rushed. It just wouldn't be very Dutch.

THE
HOMECOMING FLOAT

S itting on the piece of rectangle foam covered in a black sheet that serves as my couch (the nicest piece of furniture in my Amsterdam apartment), I open a letter from my mother written on smoke-damaged kitten-with-a-ball-of-yarn stationery that she saved from our house fire ten years prior. The envelope is sealed with a large Christmas sticker. It is late September.

It seems much has happened in Indiana since she last wrote.

In the bad news department, there was a shooting at the Earring Tree Kiosk in the Indianapolis Mall, which affected sales at Romancing the Seasons, my mother's year-round Christmas store, unfortunately situated on the same end of the mall where, as my mother puts it, "gang people buy their earrings."

In the good news department, the mystery of my always-napping sister was solved—she has been diagnosed with Epstein-Barr virus. For years she'd been napping the day away, with only a few sad attempts to wake herself to watch the news and scoop the kitty litter. Since her diagnosis, she can nap in front of the TV all day, guilt-free. She also has taught her cat to pee in the toilet.

And in news I can't decide is bad or good, only one of the five obituaries my mom enclosed with the letter is someone I actually know.

The letter ends with what is, I think, an invitation to come home for a visit: "Don't forget to take a break from what I'm sure feels like a 'fairy tale' and come back to reality for a while. We'd love to see you!"

As far as I can tell, the only fairy tale aspect of Amsterdam (besides the canal houses, the little lit-up bridges, and the talking cows) is the little troll junkie who hangs out near my apartment and who is often so full of magic he passes out with a needle dangling out of his arm.

This same morning, the troll junkie tries to scare me from crossing his bridge by standing in the middle of the bike path, screaming and pulling out his eyebrows. But since I am en route to the New Age bookstore, where I make weekly visits, I know whatever trauma I endure will soon be remedied.

I need to write back to Mom and tell her that I am already planning a trip home from Disney-dam, but that can wait. I write my three double-sided *The Artist's Way* "morning pages" in an effort to tap into my subconscious mind—where my true self lies—and I come up with some pretty astute insights.

> *Well, good morning! Here I am, doing the best I know how to do. Am I crazy or are rice cakes with cottage cheese and hot sauce on them the perfect snack?*

> *Man, I'm scared to die. And in the dream there was this little baby that I was in charge of—I think it was a baby—it felt like a baby—and I left it in a shopping cart. No, when I left it in the shopping cart it was just a sweatshirt. Anyway.*

> *Why do I keep telling everyone that I don't eat breakfast? I do eat it, I always have. Why am I ashamed?*

But I still have important work to do. I need to spend the next forty-five minutes composing what I know is a very important letter to a very important person in my life. And her name is "me."

Part of *The Artist's Way* guide for my life's journey, the letter is my spiritual task of the day. I am to ask myself for forgiveness for all that remains unforgiven from my past. This is my third time attempting the letter, and this time I really need to get all the unforgivens out—from dating the creepy twenty-two-year-old stand-up comedian when I was sixteen to buying all my bikes since I've lived in Holland from junkies. (As soon as they steal one, I go buy it back—a practice the Dutch have scolded me for so often I have to lie and claim the junkies are just friends that I lend my bike to once in a while.)

I dive into the Letter to Self one more time. I can never get past the first line.

Dear Lauren,
I'd like to say I've known you all your life
but in reality, I feel I just met you last week
at the New Age book store.

Dear Lauren,
Remember when you were so fat that kids
would "moo" at you in the hallways at
school? Well, I do.

Dear Lauren,
I hope you can read this since your hand-
writing is so shitty.

Exhausted from my morning pages and my Letter to Self, and knowing I should save some energy for my morning meditation, a quick postcard will have to suffice for Mom. My search for a working pen is interrupted by a loud voice.

"Do you see those hooks on the top of the houses?" On the street below my window, the tour guide's amplified question breaks the morning silence. "Well, when the Dutch move in or out of their homes, they use a method they've been using for centuries . . . "

The boats run all day long, right in front of my building, offering tourists a taste of historic Amsterdam. I pull my curtains back, open the windows, and plant myself in a pose that I hope looks like a Dutch girl sitting at her breakfast table, writing in her journal. I don't yet have anything to write, but the boat is right in front of my window, tourist cameras poised to snap what they believe is an intimate portrait of Dutch life. For their benefit, I fake-write a few lines with my pen just hovering above the postcard. When I hear a few excited American accents say, "Look up there!" I start fake-writing like I am Amadeus—clutching at my bangs and composing furiously.

Once the boat passes I write:

> *Dear Mom,*
> *I have a paid three-week vacation (I never*
> *got that back in "reality") and will be*
> *coming home. It starts in October. Can't*
> *wait! Love you all very much, exactly as*
> *you are.*
>
> *—Lauren*

It's time for me to go home and show my family how much living in Amsterdam has changed me. I am so different than the girl they had last seen, it's as if I've been away at rehab for two years, only with a lot of smoking and drinking. Reverse rehab.

I wish they would all come visit and see my new life in action. But they made it clear that their last big trip, a cruise to Alaska, had in their opinion been a complete bust. "I've seen more wildlife in our backyard," they like to say. They are done with traveling for a while.

Mostly I want them to see the amazing eighteenth-century canal house where I have an apartment—an apartment that is a direct reflection of how far I have progressed on my spiritual path.

It is the inkling that I would have never found my lovely home if I hadn't been a four-hundred-pound Moroccan man in a past life who died choking on his own spit that led me to my favorite spot in town—the New Age bookstore (or as

I like to call it, the I'll Never Have Another Unhappy Day Again store). Whenever I cross the threshold, hear the whales singing, and smell the myrrh burning, I know I am on the brink of discovering answers, answers, answers.

It was the past life section where I met two light and airy German girls who lived half the week at an ashram following an Indian guru with "powerful eyes," and the other half in the apartment that is now mine.

The German sari sisters had just received the news that the guru had a dream, and in that dream the two girls moved to Dallas to marry men that lived at her Texas ashram.

"Is Texas wonderful?" Gudula asked, with wide loving eyes.

I got so caught up in the way they both seemed to be bubbling with this "isn't life wondrous?!?" energy that I started talking back to them in a sort of hybrid Indian/German ashram speak.

"Oh, yes! For you shall see! Wondrous is it, this land of Texas!"

They invited me over for lavender tea and "meat that is good for your blood."

The moment I walked into the apartment I got heart palpitations. It was gorgeous. Three tall windows lined one whole wall of the main room and opened out onto a beautiful canal. So much light has never before filled an apartment more beautifully. I was ready to push them down the steps and take over the lease.

An hour later I was sitting cross-legged on the floor, wrapped in spiritual clothes, as Gudula stood behind me and pushed on the top of my head with her palm. Apparently this was a major component in the cool breeze meditation practiced at the ashram, but I had my eyes on the prize.

"Have you guys found someone to take this place when—"

"Shhhh," Florina interrupted. "Get ready!"

Gudula removed her hand and plopped herself down right in front of me. Florina plopped down next to her. Both of them had huge smiles on their faces and were so close to me I could smell their good-for-the-blood meat breath.

"Is someone from the ashram going to take it?" I asked, undaunted.

"Do you feel it?" Florina asked.

The only thing I had felt was her taking her hand off of my head. And the intense hope of moving in. Right when I was about to ask about what the total move-in cost would be they grabbed each other's little hands and intensified their anticipation. I wasn't going to get a key without celebrating my new cool breeze.

"Oh my god! That's amazing!" I yelled.

The girls started clapping and I joined in.

"Yes, the cool breeze out the top of your head! You felt it!" Gudula and Florina gave each other a hug.

I wanted to ask them if the cool breeze might have just been from the blood rushing back to where they were pressing so hard, but didn't want to put a damper on things.

It wasn't until we were all singing made-up songs to the sunset that they asked me if I would like to take the apartment when they left for the wonders of Texas.

Bowing like a level-one monk in training, I replied, "Yes, thank you. Oh, thank you."

"But first you have to come to meet the guru," Gudula insisted.

Uh-oh—if the guru was a good one, she'll take one look at me and call "bullshit." Or try to read my aura but find my colors blocked by clouds of green pot smoke.

Maybe it was more a formality. Like a meet-the-parents thing. Whatever it was, even bathing the guru's feet in goat's pee—if it meant getting the apartment, I'd do it.

That evening the girls took me to a large hall full of hundreds of followers (or possibly apartment hunters) where the guru was holding a public meditation. Unless Gudula and Florina were high-ranking followers—which they could be, as they could "cool breeze" like nobody's business—I doubted I'd have to meet the guru one-on-one.

The bulk of the evening was spent waiting for the guru, a heavyset Indian woman in a canary yellow sari, to make her way from the back of the room to her stack of pillows in the front. Ms. Guru was somewhere between the age of seventy and one hundred and ten. (The golden scarf wrapped around her head kept slipping down into her face—otherwise I could have gotten a better look.) She moved very slowly, grabbing onto the backs of chairs and any available arms as she shuffled. A few times her sari got caught on the chairs behind her, prompting her to give it an aggressive tug and whip around with a glare, "Who the hell is standing on my dress?"

When she stopped at our aisle, Gudula and Florina grabbed my arms and squeezed. I raised my eyebrows with a sort of "Well, look at that!" fake excitement and hoped the guru would suddenly find the energy to point at me and shout, "Get that woman a credit check!" But she passed right by, leaving our entire row buzzing.

"Very powerful eyes!" the crowd oohed. "Very powerful!"

The guru finally reached the stage—a miracle in and of itself. A nervous minion led her to a flapjack stack of brightly colored pillows covered in rose petals and clipped a microphone to her sari.

After she caught her breath, which took a good three minutes, the spiritual lecture began.

"The truth is the truth," she wheezed. "The TRUTH is the TRUTH. The truth IS the truth. THE truth is THE truth." Etcetera, etcetera.

When she finished speaking she remained seated on her pillow pile (where she was probably going to stay until her next session the following morning). I turned to the girls.

"It's so true," I gushed. "The truth IS the truth. I mean, the TRUTH is the truth."

The day I signed the lease, Gudula and Florina showed me a bowl of lemons and peppers. They told me to leave the bowl uncovered for four days and five nights. On the fifth day I was to throw the offering into the canal. The lemons and peppers were supposed to suck any bad energy out of the room and throwing them in canal was, Gudula added, just for fun.

As I threw the lemons and peppers into the faces of unsuspecting bikers and tourists, missing the canal entirely, I realized that this apartment was the beginning of my new life—the first step on my spiritual journey.

If I can score an amazing apartment like this at the age of twenty-three, I can't possibly be the fucked up, irresponsible, mild epileptic with poor judgment that my family has seen all these years.

Tomorrow morning I head home for three weeks. My bags are stuffed with Dutch pancake mix and syrup and a few sausages, plus Drop, the Dutch candy that tastes like dog shit mixed with asphalt—gifts for my American family.

I'd promised my mother I'd help out at Romancing the Seasons for the first week of my stay. She asked and I agreed because I thought it sounded kind of kitschy and crazy.

"I'm going home to work in a mall!" I kept telling all the Dutch people I work with at the hotel.

"Well, tell J. R. Ewing we said, 'Howdy!'" they would say back.

I'm a beloved sort of mascot for all the hard-working Dutch folks who have spent their whole lives in the service industry. I'm the little round, loud American girl. It's not uncommon when I'm preparing a tray to bring up to one of the guest rooms for me to find myself surrounded by a few cooks, a dishwasher, and someone from accounting who wandered into the kitchen to steal some food.

"I heard her laughing all the way down the hallway," one of the gathered will say. "She laughs loud. You laugh loud, you know?" Then they want to know why I do, which I can't answer, but they laugh at the funny faces I make while I feel attacked and surrounded.

When I once complained to the bartender, Rocco, about this practice of being surrounded and picked on, he looked at me quizzically.

"Everyone loves you!" he said. "They think you are a funny American girl and want to play with you!"

During this past week, I've been in a self-imposed spiritual boot camp to guarantee that my family will see who I've become, trying to get as much enlightenment in as I can before I get on the plane. I've increased my "surround those who cause you the most pain in a golden light of forgiveness" visualizations to twice a day, and every morning I've been cramming in three hours of spiritual affirmations:

> *"You are a beautiful person . . . " NO! I shouldn't say, "you," I should say "I." "I am a beautiful being . . . " A being? What am I, an alien? "I am a beautiful person . . . " That kind of sounds like I'm beautiful on the inside, but on the outside? Fucking forget about it. It's like something you'd say to someone who you found really unattractive: "No, but you're a beautiful person."*

They're not so much affirmations as discussions.

With my journey home looming in the morning, I use my break at work to hide in the dressing room and do some quick chanting on the ancient word for god ("huu"), which my healer friend, Wendy, had taught me. A transplant from Australia who lives just down the canal, Wendy told me I should chant "huuuu" in a high-pitched "this is a test of the emergency broadcast system" tone twice a day to help me summon my dream master.

I get about three minutes into heavy huu-ing when the dressing room door flies open and Rocco enters. I've had a crush on Rocco's cocky bartender ways for a long time, and I find his blatant desire to have sex with me touching. He'd heard my "huuuu" noise in the hallway and thought there was some kind of leak in the pipes. I tell him there's no leak and we start making out.

After I pick up my paycheck I catch a glimpse of him cutting up limes behind the bar and almost go over to talk to him but decide I shouldn't. My focus should not be on flirtations and boys, it should remain steadily fixed on my Trip to Bountiful—my journey home.

At 4:00 a.m. my doorbell rings and it's Rocco. "I thought I saw your light on," he yells into the intercom.

I have a major trip the next day—a spiritual quest of sorts—and my plane leaves at 11:00 a.m., so this is really obnoxious. But flattering too—he knew where I lived, and I'd never shared that with him.

I buzz him in.

After some incredibly mediocre sex we lie on my tiny mattress together. Well, he lies on it. I am half off it, gripping the side with one leg and one arm, the other half of me on my freezing concrete floor.

"You see this?" He points to his chest. "Stab wound," he says. I pull myself up onto the mattress to give it a little kiss, but then I realize I don't want to kiss a stab wound.

"How did that happen?" I ask. Suddenly the reality that I had a man named Rocco in my bed hits me. "Never mind," I say.

He gets up and moves to my couch. He lights a cigarette and sits down with his arms stretched out across the back of my couch, using his stab-wounded beer belly as a little shelf for his ashtray. He looks completely wrong in my light blue room adorned with hanging crystals and paintings of fairies kissing magical flying pigs.

He offers to buy me a new television and pay my rent. But then he cries out, "Oh, man!" and puts his head in his hands. "How I do this to Magda?" He starts crying. Magda, it turns out, is his long-term partner—not technically a wife but pretty much.

The stab wound just keeps making more and more sense.

"And you know I like you, but you're not for me," he continues. "You're not my type, you know?" He takes a drag off his cigarette.

"Shhhh, I know. I know . . . " I tell him.

And then he quickly dries up, gets his clothes on, and asks if he paid my rent could he come crash here the nights he was too drunk to ride his bike home, since I live so close to the hotel.

It's 5:00 a.m. and I have to be at the airport in four hours.

After Rocco's departure I'm not feeling well at all. In an attempt at soothing background music I play my creative visualization tape, but I can't focus on it. Why did I do this? Rocco is disgusting. I'm disgusting. My mom will never find out that I did this. But maybe she'll be able to tell. She's creepy-good at knowing everything that's going on with me. Why did I do this—throw myself off right before my trip?

I can't sleep and start to have a muscle spasm in my stomach.

This hasn't happened to me since I was in high school and was diagnosed as a "spastic diaphragm brought on by a mild petite mal seizure." It feels like I'm having the wind knocked out of me over and over again—I can't catch my breath. I'd told Wendy about these episodes and she'd said to call her the next time one happened and she'd get rid of it.

In the past I hadn't wanted other people around when I'm rolling around on the floor screaming in pain, trying to rip my clothes off. I considered it quality "me time." But now I have to get on a plane in three hours. I call Wendy and beg her to come quick.

The first thing she does is lay her hands on me, close her eyes, and let out a giant belch.

"That's you," she says. "That's your bad energy I'm releasing." Then she burps again. "Wow. You have a lot of bad energy."

A minute later she lets out a giant fart. "That's you too."

All of the burping and farting and blaming her burrito dinner on me makes me more tense, so I ask her to leave.

Before she goes she tells me that she'd seen a vision as she'd worked on me.

"Did it have something to do with acid reflux?" I ask.

"No. It's about communication. These seizures happen because you are not speaking your truth. You are not saying what you want to say." Then she has a little hiccup burp. "That one wasn't you—that was me."

Her departure brings on a wave of relaxation. Just in time to grab my luggage and head for the train station.

As I'm dragging my bags to the station the magic junkie troll from under the bridge rides by and tries to sell me my bike for twenty guilders. I don't have time to buy it back. I scream "Fuck you! That's my bike!" in English, then in Dutch, and make a note to learn how to say it in German. He screams the Dutch word for "bitch" back at me. My spiritual journey has begun.

"You'd better not dress like that when you fly anymore," my father says as we walk to baggage claim. "Makes you look like you're running drugs. I'm surprised you got through customs as fast as you did. I would have thought you were trouble, dressed all in black like that."

By the time he's sharing his secret technique of tying a bright pink ribbon on his luggage so he doesn't lose it (saying if I didn't do it next time, I'd be sorry) I am sucking back the golden light that I'd attempted to surround my family in, farting it out, and blaming them.

"Slow down, please. I'm not used to riding in cars and I feel sick!" I yell to my parents from the back seat. "Everybody rides their *fiets* in Amsterdam—I'm not used to cars." I stick my head in between the front seats. "That's so weird. Did you hear that? I said a Dutch word mixed in with English—wow, I didn't expect for that to start happening!"

Neither of them even tilts their head in my direction to feign listening. The only thing my mom says is, "Fix your seatbelt, Sid, it's all twisted up."

Four hours later we pull into our driveway and I am still trying to impress them.

"I go to the library and check out children's books in Dutch—that's how I really started learning the language. And I make these Dutch pancakes—they are so good. They're very hard to make and I do it really well—I'll make you guys some while I'm here. If you have the right pan—it takes a very special pan . . ."

I finally have the chance to show off my Dutch when my sisters and my parents start asking me how to say certain words in Dutch. But they keep picking words that are exactly the same in Dutch as in English.

"How do you say 'wind'?"

"Wind."

"How about 'water'?"

"Water."

My father gets bored and announces, "Well, I'm going to bed. Hey, I just spoke Dutch!"

The next morning I tell myself that once Mom and I are working in her store together she'll tell me how struck she is by the change in me. She always waits until we're alone to tell me what's wrong and right about me.

As soon as I come downstairs, ready to Romance the Seasons, Mom sends me back up to comb my hair.

When I tell her I did comb it she says that she has a hard time believing it's my desired hairstyle and I should go give it one more shot.

I stomp up the stairs, like I've been doing since I was nine years old, intent on styling my hair like Dorothy Hamill's. It's the only hairstyle my mother has ever really loved on me.

The woman is a dictator! She never admits to any personal weakness, ever. In almost all of our conflicts over the years she's used the "I didn't hit you, you ran into my fist" defense. And whenever I've pointed that out, she throws her head back and gives an evil cackle.

Just as I'm about to call on my higher self to guide me, I hear my mother yelling up the stairs.

"And no black. Springs shouldn't wear black. Check your palette!"

The palette she's referring to is this color analysis that she paid to have all her daughters undergo when I was in eighth grade. My best color was an institutional green. (I look amazing against the walls of hospitals and jails.) The only color clothing I brought with me is black.

Finally my mother resigns herself to the fact that this must be how they dress in Europe. But she can't help noting, "Which is sad because it washes you out."

The first thing I lay eyes on in her store is a life-size porcelain statue of a golden retriever with a big floppy sun hat and a basket of flowers in his mouth. You couldn't really put a price on a unique item like this, but if you had to, apparently that price would be four hundred dollars.

"Okay, that scares me," I say, pointing to the shiny Aryan nation puppy.

"Thank you!" my mom says in the brightest voice she can muster. She pats the golden dog on its head and tells it, "Don't worry, I love you."

Any item in the store that makes no sense to me and is completely overpriced (meaning, the entire inventory) is, according to my mother, "One of my most popular items."

"If you see the kids with the puffy coats come in the store, let me know because there's really no reason they should come in here," she advises. She fusses with the cobbler's house in Christmas Village, moving it closer to Scrooge's house.

There's no reason for anyone to come in the store, as far as I'm concerned.

"Nothing in your store *does* anything," I say. I realize by the manner in which my mother ignores what I say, that I'm pushing it.

She goes in the back and re-emerges with her hands full of teddy bears wearing little homemade outfits.

"Lauren, you are the most negative of my three daughters, and you always have been." She says this very matter-of-factly and then sets the teddy bears down in their little individual rocking chairs. "And you seem worse. What's happened to you?"

As soon as she's disappeared into the back, I pick up the bear wearing a little American flag sweater and punch him in his face.

She calls out from the back, "I saw that!" and I get a chill.

The first customer of the day enters the store wearing a sweatshirt featuring a big hippo dressed like a ballerina. Under the picture it says, "Read a book." The connection is lost on me but at this point everything is.

"Hi. I'm looking for a hippo-shaped Christmas ornament that says 'Baby's Second Christmas' on it." She states her request with such seriousness that it sounds like it's some sort of medical emergency.

But I can't answer her because my neck muscles have gone slack and my head has tumbled forward.

Luckily, my mom yells out a cheery, fake-sounding but not actually fake "Hello! Can I help you?!?" She escorts the lady to the hippo collectable section and comes back to me, still slumped over the cash register.

"CUTE!" The hippo woman screeches from across the store.

"Oh, what do you see?" my mom asks, in exactly the same way she asks the cats when they're looking out the window.

The hippo woman holds up a ceramic mouse lying on its back on a piece of cheese. His extended belly is covered in cheese crumbs and his wide-open mouth is drooling cheese.

For the next several minutes, they just scream back and forth at each other across the store.

"Cute!"

"Cute!"

"CUTE!"

"CUTE!"

"CUTE! CUTE!!!!!!!"

Finally Mom runs over to cup the little mouse figure in her hands, beaming like a proud parent.

"You know what he's called?" Mom asks. "He's called 'too pooped to party!' Now, how much does he cost?"

I'm standing right next to the price-list book but she doesn't even bother asking me, knowing how useless I'll be. She goes right to the source and asks the mouse. "How much are you?" Checking his tag she discovers he's sixty dollars. I suspect she's shocked she'd priced him so cheaply.

I pick up the cheese knife next to the cash register and try to slash my throat. But because the knife handle features a little mouse on top of a piece of cheese, the only reaction I get is, "CUTE!"

Maybe it's jet lag but I cannot muster any enthusiasm. I just sit at the cash register with a deeply crabby look on my face that doesn't change all day. The only time it even comes close to changing is when a group of ten-year-old kids comes running into the store and all start clapping loudly. At first I think it's a Boy Scout troop putting on a little show for money, but it turns out they're clapping to set off the sound-activated ghosts hanging all over the store. At the sound of a clap, the ghosts start shaking and making a high pitched "Ooooo" noise. It's not unlike my "huuuu" chant, but without the accompanying golden light it's brutal.

As soon as the ghosts stop, the kids clap again, setting them off. Everyone in the mall knows about these ghosts, and throughout the day, just as it finally gets quiet, someone sticks their head in, claps, and leave me huu-ing in hell.

Besides the ghosts, the relentless use of the word "cute," and eating muffins the size of Bundt cakes for lunch, the hardest thing about the day is my mother explaining my behavior and appearance to every customer—whether they ask about me or not.

"That's how they dress in Europe, I guess!" she says, repeatedly. Or if I fail to give a customer a receipt: "In Copenhagen you don't give receipts, I guess!"

When I correct her and tell her I live in Amsterdam, she blames that on Europe too. "I guess in Europe it's either Copenhagen or Amsterdam. It can't be both!"

While this makes no sense to me, it seems to make perfect sense to the customers, who all smile and nod in agreement.

The harsh judging I had been required to do since landing in Indiana was really making it difficult to showcase my new "ability to love" talent. But tonight I am making dinner for my entire family. Tonight is Pannekoeken Night.

Family lore has it that as a teenager I'd made Jello-O that never gelled. Many a bewildered dinner discussion was spent trying to figure out how I managed that. But now I am going to make a feast of savory and sweet Dutch pancakes everyone is going to love. And the great thing about pancakes is that you have to keep making them, thereby avoiding a great deal of the dinner table discussion.

"Lauren, can I get another apple one?" my sister calls sleepily from the table.

"Why yes, you can! Any other orders?" I ask, doing my family pancake–making dance in the kitchen. The *pannekoeken* are coming out perfectly—thin and crepelike. Perfect.

"She can't balance a checkbook or remember her house key to save her life," my dad chimes in, "but she sure can make some pancakes, can't she!" He polishes off another sausage delight.

This moment is not about pancakes. It is about me giving of myself unto them—doing something that is entirely not about me. And as I watch my family using way too much syrup, I realize I'd been thinking about them every moment of the day in Amsterdam. That with everything I did, I'd imagine them watching me do it. Approving or disapproving (mostly disapproving), but they were with me.

"Mom's choking!" my sister yells, interrupting my reverie.

I run to the table and find that, sure enough, my mom is choking on her apple pancake.

We all freeze and watch her for a moment. But when we finally realize that wishing the moment away isn't working, someone takes action—the person most concerned for my mother: my mother. She reaches her finger into her throat and sends a piece of pancake flying out of her mouth.

As the whole family—still shaken—clears their plates away, my mother breaks the silence.

"Lauren, I'm awfully proud of you for making it on your own over there. I just wish I'd told you sooner so you wouldn't have tried to kill me with those Danish pancakes."

The next day Mom and I return to Romancing the Seasons. We are both quiet on the drive to the mall, perhaps due to last night's brush with matricide. ("How was your vacation?" "Well, I killed my mom with a *pannekoeken,* so that was awkward. From now on I'm going to put two eggs in the batter—do you think that's too eggy?")

As Mom opens and readies the store, I notice how she hums softly to the Perry Como Christmas music and deeply inhales the Glade evergreen room freshener. This shop is her New Age bookstore. In the calm before the customers arrive, my mother gazes at the Santa doorstops and Rudolph's-head coasters and sees nothing but answer, answer, answer.

ARE YOU
MY MOTHER?

I t was lunchtime at Grandview Elementary School in Indianapolis and I scanned the sea of fellow first graders to pick whom to sit next to. I chose Billy Randolph because our striking similarities lead me to believe that we may be long-lost kin. Judging by his skin tone, Billy appeared to be kind of black and kind of white. Just like me.

As soon as I sat down next to him, he curled an arm around his tater tots to guard them from me.

"Hey, I'm kinda black and kinda white, like you," I told him.

"No, you're not," he said. He pointed at Shawna, the blondest, whitest girl in the first grade. Shawna was so pale you could see her delicate organs working hard to keep her alive under paper-thin skin. Nobody ever wanted to invite Shawna to birthday parties because she was allergic to milk, sugar, grass, and air, and she always arrived with her own allergy-friendly birthday cake and a special mat to sit on.

"You look just like her," Billy said, "but fatter."

But Shawna and I looked nothing alike. Sure, I had blonde hair and blue eyes and white skin, but I didn't look like that.

The next day at lunch I sat next to Rachel Fishman.

"I'm Jewish, like you," I told her.

Wendy was at least open to the possibility. "But you don't go to temple. I've never seen you there," she said.

I told her I go every Saturday but I sat in the back. I thought I was doing okay until she waved a giant saltine cracker in front of my face.

"What's this? What's it called?" she demanded.

My answer—"a Jewish cracker"—made her so mad she turned me in to the lunchroom attendant for saying "mean things about Jewish people."

"I would never do that! I'm Jewish!" I insisted. I continued to defend myself as I was transferred to Shawna's table.

Shawna wasn't eating. She had her head down, practically lying on the table, as she drew pictures of a world she'd never know—a world where big, sugary cupcakes sit in a field of pollen-heavy grass.

"I wish I was in this picture," she said, holding up her magical dreamland.

"Well, you can't be," I told her. "You'd throw up and pass out and die."

Shawna nodded her head slowly, still coloring green for grass. "Yep," she said. "That's exactly right. You must have allergies too."

Besides the fact that I'd never had allergies—that wasn't interesting enough for me—I knew Shawna wasn't my long-lost sister because she was too similar to my real sister, or at least, my sister in my adopted family. Elizabeth didn't have allergies but she did have thyroid disease, which exempted her from gym class and somehow was connected to her love of stamp collecting.

In the third grade my teacher, Ms. Hart, announced, "Today we're going to do family trees." She wrote the word "heritage" on the chalkboard in her loopy script, and before she got to "tage," I was on my feet with my hand in the air.

"I'm adopted! I'm adopted!" I screamed, with such intensity that the other kids in the class whipped around to see if it was some special way of saying, "I'm on fire! I'm on fire!"

When Ms. Hart explained what being adopted means, someone in the back of the class yelled out, "Gross!"

"It's not gross," she said, "It's a wonderful thing. Lauren has a family that wanted her very much and therefore she has a family tree." Ms. Hart handed me the ditto sheet with the empty tree for me to fill in.

"No, I'm adopted. I have no trees," I said. Then I made a sad clown face and stared out the window at the barren landscape. "Sigh."

The mystery of my origins was endlessly fascinating to me. While my parents could account for my sister's whereabouts every day of her life so far, nobody knew where I had been the first eight days of my life. This didn't prevent my sister from theorizing, however. "Just lying there in the trash can, looking at stuff," she'd often posit.

My beloved grandmother said she hadn't wanted any direct skin-on-skin contact with me when I first arrived on the scene. "Back then nobody knew what kind of germs you might have, and I didn't know if your mom had a chance to really wash you off yet," she explained. "I made them put you on the floor on one of the dog towels."

She also made sure to point out that my biological parents could have dropped me right before they handed me to my new parents and had just acted as if nothing had happened. "They do it at the grocery store with the apples all the time."

Since my early history was so murky, every person I came into contact with was a potential family member. After the first-grade Easter party at school, I threw up in the hallway (due to the stress of the egg hunt). By the time the janitor was done cleaning up after me, I was convinced he was my real father. His misdiagnosed dyslexia and love of harmonica seemed oddly familiar. Plus he had messy hair, which I had almost every day when I first woke up. The similarities were eerie.

My real mother, I once concluded, was the newscaster on our local TV station. All of Indiana loved her and marveled at her beauty and poise. She was the most beautiful woman I was exposed to on a daily basis. The similarities between us—the hair that grew out of the top of her head, the two eyes and the skin covering all of her body—were so uncanny that watching the news was like looking in a mirror.

By middle school—perhaps well before—nobody wanted to hear about my being adopted anymore, which left me no choice but organized religion. I was forced to join the local Protestant church to get a fresh audience.

When the minister announced, "We're passing around a sign-up sheet for the annual Thanksgiving dinner, so put down your last name and how many members are in your family," I wrote in, "Weedman, family of 1," and passed it down the row.

Before the sermon was over someone had passed me a note saying, "Lauren, please join us for dinner. Love, The Ernest family of 8."

As the church started emptying out, Mrs. Ernest motioned me over to join her family. I didn't waste any time—I made a few church-appropriate jokes about the minister's haircut to endear myself and took notes on how the Ernests dressed so I could begin to blend in more easily.

"What does your family think about you being here all alone every Sunday?" Mrs. Ernest asked, with such deep concern I started to worry she was going to call child protective services.

"They know but they don't care," I said. "I tried to get them to come to church to gain a sense of fellowship, but my dad's always like, 'No, you go ahead—your mom and I are busy putting chains and locks on our bedroom doors to keep you out.'" I followed up this revelation with a face that said, "Pretty crazy, huh?"

"What? Locks and chains?" Mrs. Ernest said. "Are you being funny?"

"Only to survive, only to survive," I told her. I gestured toward the picture of Jesus on the front of the hymnal, as if to say, "This guy knows what I'm talking about."

Truth be told, the chains and the locks hadn't appeared until everyone in the family had had enough of me spending every day after school milling about in their rooms. I'd try on their clothes, dip into their beauty products, and, most importantly, search for clues about who these people were. The things I really wanted to find—diaries, anything sex-related, personal letters—were never found. Which only made me hungrier for something graphic and gritty.

Mrs. Ernest was understandably shocked by what I was saying, so I told her more.

"Every night I see them enter the combinations to unlock the locks. They think I'm watching to decipher the code, so they block the locks with their hands. Isn't that insane? Like I could tell from across the hallway '2 left, 19 right.'"

What I didn't mention to the Ernest family was that the reason I didn't try to crack the code was because it was so much easier to just get a screwdriver and take the entire door off its hinges. Once I'd wrenched the door off and set it against the wall, I could continue my most urgent search unhindered—the search for the secret file.

I was certain that somewhere in the house was hidden a file that held all the information about my birth parents. I had thought about it so much I could see the contents: photos and facts and perhaps half of a heart-shaped golden locket. I knew it was somewhere in our house.

Despite the Ernests' surprise at my revelation, they began including me in their celebrations and holidays as a "special family member." They did feel like family to me. Right down to the tension that arose at the dinner table whenever I'd excuse myself to use the restroom.

It was during one of these strained moments that the Ernests' sixteen-year-old daughter complained (in a voice she knew was loud enough for me to hear all the way upstairs in her closet), "She'd better not be sneaking into my bedroom! And searching for the other half of her locket and messing up my sweater drawer again!"

At that point I decided it was better to confine my relationship with the Ernests to the church, where they had to be nice to me or they'd go to hell.

In high school I tried not to dwell on my missing birth mother, keeping my focus instead on sex and Weight Watchers portioning. But my best friend Jill Schenburg wouldn't let me forget it.

"Ask your mom about your real mom!" she often urged. "Just ask her!"

In one particular instance, Jill was pestering me from the back seat of her car. We were both lying on the floor—me in the front, her in the back—smoking Benson & Hedges Menthol 100s between classes. (Nothing to see here, folks, just an empty car in the school parking lot with smoke pouring out the windows.)

"How can you not want to know? I'd be going crazy!" Jill repeated, for the millionth time. "Just ask your mom if she has any information she's never told you!"

"I don't want to hurt her feelings," I said. "Or make her think I'm not grateful. I at least need to wait until I'm not grounded. Everyone's mad at me right now."

Jill sat up, threw her cigarette out the window, and lit another one. She wanted to skip our next class to get breakfast at Shoney's Breakfast Bar Buffet, and she wanted me to come with her. It didn't take much to convince me. Driving out of the parking lot, both of us ducked down in the car so it appeared the car was driving itself away from school. We had a good laugh at that, and then Jill grabbed my hand and said, "You know you're a Jew. I guarantee you're going to find out you're a Jew."

That night, my mother and I prepared dinner together in the kitchen. She was grilling lamb patties for the slender members of the family (everyone but me) and I was thawing my own Weight Watchers ravioli in the microwave.

"Lauren, don't stand with your mouth wide open in front of the microwave," my mother scolded.

I hadn't realized my mouth was open. My diet left me so hungry, the ravioli-scented radiation blowing out of the microwave must've seemed like a snack.

My mother always tended to scare the shit out of me. "Give her a break," Elizabeth would snap, when I complained about how strict I thought Mom was. "Grandma tied Mom to a tree when she was little," she'd say, by way of explanation. I used to wonder if this was just a family myth or if it was just harder to find babysitters back then.

But as I watched Mom scrape the lamb patties off the grill and flip them over, I could see how truly angry she was. It was as if she hated that lamb. As if that lamb couldn't remember its house key day after day, just like me.

Tonight was not a good night to ask her about my birth mother. I did it anyway.

"Mom, can I ask you a question?" My heart was beating like I had just escaped having my ass kicked. Or was about to have it handed to me.

She tossed the lamb patties on a platter and gave me a dirty look. "What is it?" she said.

Suddenly I could see everything she was probably mad at me about—that twenty-dollar bill gone missing from her purse, the fact that I smoked not just cigarettes but pot, and that she kept paying for diets that didn't work.

"What do you want, Lauren?" And now she was also mad at me for waiting so long to ask my question. The buildup was too much and I was tempted to say never mind, but I knew that could sound suspicious. Too suspicious.

"You've got two more seconds," my mother said.

I took a deep breath. "I want to ask you about my real mom."

I did it. It took eighteen years for me to pop the question, but I did it.

The look on my mom's face was one I'd never seen before. It retained its anger but gained a sort of hurt too. This was my worst nightmare—to hurt her. In fact, I didn't think it was possible. Even when she was physically hurt, her predominant expression was anger. ("Dammit, I twisted my ankle!") So I had stolen from her, lied to her, talked smack about her behind her back, and now this.

"Lauren, I am your real mom," she said, clearly and directly. She turned around and started putting the napkins on the table.

"You know what I mean," I said. "I mean my biological parents." This was good. I was able to continue and not get too flustered.

She didn't answer my question and instead sent me to gather everyone for dinner. Which took a little while—Elizabeth was in her bedroom so she had to re-chain her door.

Picking at the crust of my Weight Watchers meal, I figured that was that, so I was surprised when my mom raised the subject again at the table.

"Is this why you've been going to Hebrew school?" she asked. "Do you think you're Jewish? Because you're not. They don't give Jewish babies away like that. You have to go through the Jewish Community Center and it's a very long process. Did Jill Schenburg tell you that you were Jewish?" She pronounced Schenburg with her interpretation of how a Jewish person talks—half screaming.

"No," I lied. "I was curious if you had a file somewhere with information that maybe you hadn't—"

"And how did you get into the black student union, Lauren? Don't you have to be black?" my Dad asked.

I wasn't technically *in* the union, I had just attended a few of their events.

At the end of the night my mom knocked once on my bedroom door and threw it open before I could say "come in" or "go away." (Not only did my door have no locks, it barely closed all the way.)

"You want to know what you are, Lauren?!?" She had a huge grin on her face like she'd lost her mind.

"Do you want to know?" the scary lady asked again.

I nodded my head silently, stunned by her freaky energy. I was sure she was going to shove a black-and-white photo in my face, one depicting my real family fighting over a can of beans. ("The one holding the can is your daddy, and the little girl holding the spoon, why that's your mama!")

But instead, she threw her empty hands into the air. "You are what we are!" she said. She was so pleased with her answer that she repeated it. "That's exactly what you are!"

Before I had a chance to ask what we were (besides white and Midwestern) she closed the door and was gone.

The next morning when I went down for breakfast I discovered that the fridge had been adorned with a Dear Abby column. The heading was "Don't Search for Me." It was a letter from a birth mother begging her birth daughter to not try to come look for her. "You'll just bring up all the pain from the time when I had to give you away," wrote Leave Me Alone in Alabama. "There is a reason why I gave you away. Please respect that."

Mom had clearly been saving this letter to argue her case when the time came. As I joined Elizabeth at the breakfast table I decided I would try to be happy with the family I had.

"I can't eat my breakfast while you eat yours," I announced to my sister. "You love your milk too much. It's gross. It's milky."

"Well, you're fat," Elizabeth countered. "So stop borrowing my clothes and stretching them all out."

We sat in silence for a while until Elizabeth shuffled to the sink in her slippers to rinse out her bowl. Before she left the kitchen she said in an odd, singsongy voice that was not hers, "I consider you my real sister and I always have, okay?"

It sounded so inauthentic I wouldn't have been surprised if my mom had been standing around the corner holding up a giant cue card and pointing to the words. ("I CONSIDER YOU MY REAL SISTER . . . ")

Senior year of high school Jill and I were smoking pot in her basement, getting ready to watch each other lip-synch to songs set on the wrong speed. She loaded her *Yentl* record (33⅓ rpm) and tried to lip-synch to it at 45 rpm. I was having the time of my life until she brought up my real mom again.

"Call the place where they adopted you and ask them," she suggested. "Maybe all you have to do is ask!" She was yelling over Barbra Streisand's chipmunked voice singing "Papa, Can You Hear Me?"

My mother had always told the story of how she chose to adopt like this: "Well, I was volunteering at the Children's Bureau because a bunch of ladies I knew from the swim club enjoyed it there—it was a nice, social place—and when I found out they did adoptions I thought, 'Oh, I'll take one.'"

When I revealed to Jill that my agency was called the Children's Bureau, she ran upstairs to get the phone book. She found the listing almost immediately and dialed the number. "I'll say I'm you," she offered helpfully. And she did.

The person on the phone told her that they couldn't release any information, but that there was an adoption support group for state-adopted adoptees that met in a local library every Tuesday night.

The next Tuesday night I was there in the adoptee circle with my mom sitting right next to me. She was the only adoptive mother in the group. The rest of the circle was made up of guilt-ridden birth mothers and eighteen-year-old adopted girls who had already had two kids of their own just so they could "have somebody who looked like me." (I counted this as the best reason to have a baby, right behind "to have something to cuddle with.")

When my mom had announced she was coming with me, I thought, "Great! Now all I need is some rope and a good strong tree." I had no idea why she suddenly wanted to come along. She clearly wasn't into my finding my birth mother, and we never did anything together besides negotiate the terms of my punishments.

When it was my turn to introduce myself and say why I was there, I felt incredibly awkward having the mom I was trying to trade in sitting right next to me. The custom was for we adoptees to announce our birthday first, then pause a moment in case one of the searching birth mothers shouted, "Bingo!" and claimed us.

"March 5, 1969," I said. There were no takers (for which, looking around the room, I thanked god), so I continued. "I'm just here because I'm adopted and it sounded kind of interesting." But before I could finish my introduction my mom jumped in with her own.

"I'm Sharon Weedman and I'm Lauren's mom," she said, smiling. "Her adoptive mother." She paused there for applause and she actually got it. We were the first adoptive mother/daughter team they'd had in a long time, apparently. The rest of the hour was spent with everyone gushing all over the rare and intense loving bond that my mother and I obviously shared.

My mother was the belle of the ball. She reached out and clasped hands with teary birth mothers, assuring them that somewhere their babies were being loved.

I sat still and quiet. I was saving all my words for the car ride home. I'd let her have her little moment in the sun—she could take over my support group for one night. But that would be it. From here on out I wanted to go alone.

"I'm dropping you at home and then I'm going back out," my mom informed me as soon as we got in the car. The shock blew my prepared speech right out of my head.

"What? Where are you going?"

"Jim—the guy with the moustache who was adopted in Arkansas—told me there's an underground search group that meets at Pizza Hut on 71st."

Before I could ask any questions she pushed me out of the car and sped off to Pizza Hut.

The next day I was minding my own business, watching twelve consecutive hours of television, when my mom walked into the family room dressed like a crazy wig lady. She was wearing a blonde wig, huge owl sunglasses, and a raincoat. The mere sight of her made me want to cry.

"What are you doing, Mom?" I asked, fighting back my panic. "Whatever you're doing—please stop. Please."

"I'm undercover!" she announced, thrusting one of her little arms up into the air in a triumphant gesture.

"No!" I screamed. I didn't understand exactly what she was doing, but all I could think was, NOOO!

"Yes!" she shouted back.

When I pleaded with her to please stop and to get some kind of professional help she threw back her head and cackled. Before I could shoot her with a tranquilizer dart, she was gone.

I called my dad and told him to keep a lookout for her on his way home from work—she was probably on the side of the road collecting Coke cans as evidence and dusting stop signs for fingerprints.

When Mom returned that evening, she explained where she had gone and why her being undercover was so important. She was breaking the law, she said, so she had to be careful. My little ballet-teaching, working-in-a-jewelry-store, lamb patty–cooking mother was out breaking the law, dressed up like Groucho Marx.

Earlier in the day, she'd gone to Terre Haute High School and asked to look through all the yearbooks from 1967 through 1969. It turned out that when I was first handed over, the adoption agency had given my mom a few basic details, which she'd scribbled down on a little piece of paper. She knew I had been born in Terre Haute, Indiana, to a fifteen-year-old boy and sixteen-year-old girl. But that was all she had to go on—that and the agency's assurance that the teen parents both came from families just full of doctors and nurses. Apparently that was the only profession the volunteer handling our adoption could think of that sounded impressive. ("Doctors and nurses—the whole lot of them. Lots of awards and thick heads of hair.")

My newly insane mother also revealed that while viewing the yearbooks she'd torn out page after page to take home and study.

"What's next?" I asked my mom. "Murder, kidnapping?"

She took her sunglasses off. "You wanted to find out about your real mother, didn't you? Well, I'm going to help you," she said, tightening the belt of her trench coat.

When I was in sixth grade my parents had planned a child-free vacation in the Bahamas. The cruise ship was scheduled to head straight through the middle of the Bermuda Triangle, so before they set sail my mother sat my sister and me down to go over her will.

"Now, girls," she said, "there's a clause in my will that says if something happens to me that it's okay with you two—if you agree—that I come back and visit you as a ghost."

She was completely serious. I think. Or else it was an elaborate joke that she constructed just to mortify me. I could never be sure. But as I watched her make such a big production of her undercover search—running out of the house for late-night meetings at the Pizza Hut with the assistant PI she'd picked up at the support group—it made me wonder if she was actually doing the search or if this was another ruse intended to get a reaction out of me. After all, pulling this one over would've guaranteed hours of family entertainment.

A week after she had ripped the pages out of the year-books, I discovered my mother calling every blonde who had graduated from Terre Haute High School in 1968. She was wearing her undercover outfit even though she was on the phone. She was reading from a script on her lap like a bad actor:

"Oh, hello, my name is Ruth Robison. I'm from the Terre Haute Alumni Association, and we're calling all of our alumni to see how they enjoyed their education with us. Did you enjoy your education? Good. Now I have a quick question. Do you remember any of your female classmates being absent from school six to nine months, due to an illness or a pregnancy?"

That was the point at which they'd usually hang up on her.

"This has nothing to do with me, Mom," I said, as she dialed the next name on her list.

"Oh, hello, my name is Ruth Robison," she said into the receiver.

The search, which coincided suspiciously with the debut of *Murder, She Wrote,* continued through my entire senior year of high school and into my first year of college.

It ebbed and flowed. At one point Mom was certain she'd found her, and that she was Asian. During dinner, everyone kept staring at me—looking for it. By dessert, we all agreed there was something vaguely Asian about me. My eyes did slant down a bit at the edges. But what about my black booty, the group wondered. How could Asian heritage explain that? And what about my Irish pores?

The search was briefly interrupted by my grandmother's death. When I tried to point out the poignancy to my mother—"Here you are, searching for my mother and you've lost your own mother"—she accused me of being overly sentimental and sent me to the bowling alley across the street from the funeral home to pick up mixed drinks for everybody.

Later, my mother's search extended to appearances on the local TV news.

"My daughter just wants to see a picture of her birth parents," she pleaded to the cameras. "Please. Again, the birth date is March 5, 1969."

It was as if I'd gone missing, even though I was seated next to her, looking irritated.

Finally I asked my mother not to tell me all the details about the search. It was too much. My heart couldn't take all the "great leads" that turned out to be false hopes.

"Don't tell me it's her until you know it's her," I begged my mom. "And I mean you *know* it's her."

Two years later, I was working as a hostess at a bar and grill famous for its high-backed booths. I had graduated from high school and gone to college, but after a bad year I had returned to Indianapolis in an attempt to figure out what to do next.

One night the phone at the hostess stand rang. "Arthur's Bar and Grill, can I help you?" I answered, trying not to sound as bored as I was.

It was my mom, who never called me at work. I wasn't even aware she knew where I worked.

"LAUREN, THE EAGLE HAS LANDED!" she yelled. "HE'S LANDED! I GOT HER! COME HOME RIGHT NOW! I GOT HER!" She was talking so loudly that the party of five waiting to be seated asked me who "her" was.

I told them it was a fishing thing and asked to leave work early.

When I opened the front door to my parents' house the first thing I heard was my mother screaming, "WE GOT HER!!"

As she told me what had happened in the last twenty-four hours, I stood over the sink shoving handful after handful of stale microwave popcorn in my face. I didn't bother to shut my mouth or swallow—I just chewed furiously and took in her story.

Continuing her life of crime, my mom had bribed Jim, the Pizza Hut committee member, who conveniently worked in a hospital, to go into the state records and see what he could find. He had typed my name into the computer and my birth mother's name had come right up. He called my mother immediately and gave her the name: Diane McQuillen.

My mother researched McQuillens who lived in the area where I was born and discovered the only current listing was an Emily and David McQuillen. When she felt it was getting too hot ("too close to the flame"), she handed the information to her assistant PI, Jim, whom she'd been working closely with over the years and trusted.

Jim called the McQuillens, posing as an insurance man who needed to contact Diane. Sure enough, Emily and David were Diane's parents. Suspecting that the nervous man on the other end of the phone was not who he said he was, they offered to call their daughter on his behalf and give his number to her. Emily hung up and immediately called Diane, who now lived in Denver.

"She's back," Emily said to Diane. "The baby has come back."

At this point I was feeling incredibly relieved that nobody had threatened to shoot anybody for "meddling in their personal business." And it was happening. After so many dead ends, the answers were just flowing and flowing. And if things kept going like this, I knew I'd soon be talking to my birth mother, and that was something I'd never allowed myself to imagine. So for the moment I just tried to wait and see what was next.

My mom continued her story: Diane, who was at work when she got the call, snuck to a pay phone and called Jim back.

"This is Diane," she said. "My parents told me you were looking for me?"

"Yes," Jim said. "Does the date March 5, 1969, mean anything to you, Diane?"

It did. It was the day her parents re-mortgaged their farm. It was also the day she had a baby. Diane was my mother.

After making the initial contact, Jim had set up a time for my mother and me to call Diane: that same night. My mother was sharpening pencils and prepping questions from her research notebooks—as if she was sure Diane was going to jump on board, thrilled to be found and be reminded of her sordid past.

"Did you ever think that maybe I was a product of some incest/rape situation that maybe she doesn't want to be reminded of?" I asked my mom.

"Well, the inbred thing has crossed our minds quite a bit," Mom said. "But I doubt she'd be so eager to talk to us if there was some big trauma."

I thought she was being so naive. I suspected that Diane agreed to arrange the call so she could tell us to once and for all leave her alone. "There is a reason why I gave her up—please respect that reason," she'd explain. Then she'd refer us to her letter published in Dear Abby.

I changed my mind. I didn't want to make the call. "What if we can't understand her?" I asked my mom. I remembered the yellowed column stuck on the fridge: *Signed, Leave Me Alone in Alabama.*

"I'm pretty sure she speaks English," my mom said. She already had the receiver in her hand and was getting ready to dial.

"No, I mean, because she's missing half her teeth and has a mouth full of chewing tobacco . . . "

Mom finished dialing and put the phone to her ear. My dad was in the next room, watching a repeat of *The Rockford Files.* But sensing something big was happening in the house, he switched it off and just sat in his chair looking toward the kitchen. I held on to the counter so I didn't start shaking.

My mom was beaming, until someone on the other end of the line answered. Then her face fell and I could see how scared she was.

In the smallest voice I'd ever heard her use, she said, "Hello? Diane? Hello. My name is Sharon Weedman and I'm calling about Lauren. I'm her mom. I mean, you're her mom!"

I could hear Diane's laugh coming through the phone, and that was it. My mom started laughing too, and continued with what she now saw as a hilarious joke: "No! You're her mother!"

The "No, you are!"s went back and forth for a while before my mom got serious and picked up her pencil. She wanted to get some solid facts for the book she was working on, called *I Searched . . . I Found!*

Mom's excitement was so sweet and intense that I worried she'd thank Diane for the information and hang up. She told Diane that in the book she would refer to her as my "BM" (birth mother).

"BM! Right! You're her BM! Ha ha ha!" she giggled into the phone. "Oh, Lauren's giving me a dirty look. She doesn't like the term 'bowel movement' so I usually say 'BM,' which she hates even more. Now, Diane, do you like to eat? Because Lauren sure does. We just can't get her out of the kitchen. In fact she's in the kitchen right now! Yes. She's standing right in front of me."

Suddenly she seemed to notice I had been standing there the entire time.

"Oh, Diane," she said, looking at me. "Thank you so much. She's just great. We've just had a lot of fun with her. Did you want to talk to her?"

I clenched up, worried that Diane might say, "No thanks, but tell her I said, 'Hi.'" It was possible that my mother had already worn her out, and that I would end up with a Hallmark card and five bucks' back-allowance.

"Well hold on, I'll put her on!" my mother said.

She told me to pick up the phone in the other room. I was hoping for a little more privacy, but since I'd been the one breaking into people's rooms all my life, I doubted I'd earned it.

When I picked up the phone in the library, my mom's voice came blasting out. "So when is your birthday? Do you have any diabetes in the family?"

Just when I was about to give up on ever getting a chance to say something, my dad walked into the kitchen.

"Oh my god, Sid's in the kitchen too, now!" Mom screamed into the phone. "Wow, this is a big night!"

I wasn't sure my dad knew I was adopted, much less what all this excitement was about. But I heard him gently ask my mom to hang up so that I could have a chance to say hello. Hearing him ask her that made me so sad I almost wanted to hang up too.

When Mom finally did hang up, Diane and I sat on the phone for a few seconds in silence. It was too much, I thought. It was way too much.

All my life, whenever I watched television shows that featured a birth scene, I'd feel sorry for myself. I couldn't help thinking that at the moment I was born, instead of an outpouring of love and a counting of toes there was a whisking away of Baby Jane Doe to avoid the pain and the shame. Finally, this could be the celebration I'd always suspected I had been denied. Or it could just as easily not be.

But when I first heard the sound of her voice it became very simple.

Diane didn't sound ashamed or angry or inbred. (Or—sadly—Jewish.) She sounded real.

"Well hi, Lauren," Diane said in the sweetest voice I'd ever heard. "This is a pretty exciting phone call, huh?"

ACKNOWLEDGMENTS

It's a cliché but I have to say it—if it wasn't for my editor Brangien Davis, this book would not have been possible. She worked so hard with me the entire time and I am very grateful.

And the following people also were key supportive folks who were so good to me I almost feel guilty ('cuz I talk shit behind their backs all the time—just kidding). Deep thanks to:

Jeff Weatherford

Zach Weatherford

Christie Smith

David Weatherford

Heidi Lenze

Wendy Spero

Jon Bernstein

Matt Price and
Eric Friedman at
Show and Tell

Maggie Rowe and
Jaclyn Lafer from
Sit and Spin

Jill Soloway

Dave Eggers

Kurt Stephan

Gary Luke

Jacque, Kaz, and
Casa Earl

Mike Hoffman,
Samantha Silva,
Olivia, Atticus, and
Phoebe

ABOUT THE AUTHOR

Photo: Tracey Melville

Lauren Weedman made her television debut on Comedy Central's Emmy Award–winning *The Daily Show with Jon Stewart* in 2001 as a featured correspondent. At the same time, Lauren was a regular on NPR's national political satire show *Rewind* and appeared Off Broadway in her solo show *Homecoming* at the Westside Theatre in New York City. For two years, Lauren was also a cast member for the long-running local-turned-national comedy show *Almost Live* for Comedy Central and guest starred on several episodes of *Reno 911!*

Prior to her television work, she studied, wrote, and performed in Amsterdam for five years. Lauren returned to the States with her first play *Homecoming*, which began as a 15-minute performance art piece that ultimately grew into a full-length show. She also toured with the Seattle Repertory Theatre.

Later that year, *Homecoming* was featured at HBO's U.S. Comedy Arts Festival in Aspen, Colorado, before finding its way Off Broadway. *Homecoming* earned Lauren the honor of being published in *Women Playwrights: The Best Plays of 2002*. In Fall 2002, the Empty Space Theatre in Seattle premiered her solo work *Rash*, which was recognized by the *Seattle Times'* Footlight Awards, with nods for both "Best New Play" and "Best Solo Performance."

Rash received tremendous reviews, including: "Weedman comes so very close to celebrating indulgence rather than just contemplating it that when she manages to do both things at once, it's dizzyingly brilliant: She ends up hitting all her targets—including herself" (*Seattle Weekly*) and "Since first turning up on Seattle stages in the early 1990s, Lauren Weedman has proved herself one terrifically funny gal. And more people know that since she moved to New York two years ago and earned some well-deserved breaks in TV and Off Broadway" (*Seattle Times*).

Other solo shows include *Amsterdam*, *If Ornaments Had Lips*, and *Wreckage*. Her latest play—*Bust*—about her work as a volunteer at the Los Angeles County Jail, was named "Best of Theatre" by *Seattle Magazine* in 2006.

Lauren is also the recipient of a 2007 Alpert/MacDowell Fellowship.

She currently lives in Los Angeles and is developing a pilot for Oxygen TV based on her Web series *Our Bodies, Myself*.